Models ~for~ Writing

Teacher's Book

4

Chris Buckton

Anne Sanderson

Series editor: Leonie Bennett

GINN

Author Team Chris Buckton
Anne Sanderson
Series editor: Leonie Bennett

Bill Ball (Scottish 5–14 Guidelines)
Robert Hunter (Northern Ireland Curriculum)
Beverley Parker and Steve Yates (ICT)

Ginn
Linacre House, Jordan Hill, Oxford, OX2 8DP
a division of Reed Educational and Professional Publishing Ltd
www.ginn.co.uk

Ginn is a registered trademark of Reed Educational and Professional Publishing Ltd

ISBN 0602 296854

04 03 02 01
10 9 8 7 6 5 4 3 2

Designed and produced by Gecko Ltd, Bicester, Oxon
Cover design by Gecko Ltd, Bicester, Oxon
Printed in the UK by Ashford Colour Press, Hampshire.

Contents

Introduction

Welcome to *Models for Writing*, the first complete programme to deliver Shared, Guided and Extended writing at Key Stage 2 in line with the requirements of the National Literacy Strategy framework. This programme links writing inside the Literacy Hour with extended writing outside the hour in a structured way. *Models for Writing* offers thorough coverage of the NLS writing objectives (*see matching chart on page 10*).

It also covers the requirements of the Scottish Guidelines on English Language 5 – 14 (1991), and the Northern Ireland Curriculum (1996) (*see correlation charts on pages 11 and 12*).

Improving Children's Writing

Models for Writing will help you to improve your pupils' writing across the ability range, bringing as many pupils as possible up to level 4 by the end of year 6.

It helps to improve writing through:

- stimulating model texts that interest and excite pupils
- modelled writing sessions which provide children with a clear structure
- differentiated activities and extended writing
- guided writing sessions that focus on both text and sentence level work.

Differentiation

Differentiation is offered in group and guided activities in the **Pupil's Book**. The activities are flagged with the following symbols:

1 Work for **lower attainers**, often supported by a photocopy master.

2 Work for the whole class. **Lower attainers** are often supported by a photocopy master such as a writing frame.

3 Work for **higher attainers**.

The lesson plans for each unit (*see pages 38–97*) offer specific guidance on how to work with different attaining groups during Guided writing.

Assessment

Models for Writing helps you to assess children's writing and judge how their skills are developing. You will find guidelines on assessment and annotated samples of children's writing at different levels on pages 22–31.

SAT Preparation

Suggestions for which units to use to practise writing under timed conditions are offered on pages 35–37.

Information and Communication Technology

Models for Writing includes a comprehensive section of ICT activities for each unit (*see pages 102–108*).

In the lesson plans, the ICT symbol indicates when an ICT activity could be used for that unit, and cross-references you to the appropriate page in the ICT section.

Structure/Components

Models for Writing has a simple structure which links Shared and Guided writing in the Literacy Hour with extended writing outside of the Hour.

Each Year of *Models for Writing* has:

Pupil's Book containing model texts, guided and supported activities, and extended writing.

Pupil's Book

Teacher's Book offering lesson plans for each unit, curriculum matching charts, assessment guidance, and ICT activities.

Teacher's Book

Overhead Transparencies of model texts and writing frames for whole class teaching.

Colour Overhead Transparancies

Photocopy Masters for differentiation and homework.

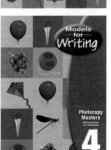

Photocopy Masters

How to use *Models for Writing*

When to Use *Models for Writing*

Each unit is designed around two lessons, with an additional extended writing session. You can use **Models for Writing** alongside any other literacy programme by slotting the two lessons into your planning. Alternatively, you could choose to spend more time on a particular unit or theme (*see 'Linked Units' below*) and extend the lessons over a whole week. Each unit focuses on a single writing objective, making it easy for you to see where they fit into your teaching, and making **Models for Writing** an extremely flexible programme.

How each unit works

Models for Writing is made up of 30 units. In each unit you will find:

LESSON ONE: MODEL TEXT

- The first lesson focuses on the study of a short model text from the **Pupil's Book**. (The text provides the model for the next lesson's writing.) Where annotation of the text is required, it is also offered on an OHT.

- Differentiated group activities are offered through the **Pupil's Book** and the **Photocopy Masters**.

LESSON TWO: WRITING

- *Shared Writing* – Shared or modelled writing based on the model text. Writing or planning frames are offered as OHTs where needed.

- *Guided, Group and Independent Writing* – Differentiated group and guided activities. Guidance is given on which group to work with during the guided writing session.

EXTENDED WRITING

- Each unit ends with a suggested extended writing activity, to be completed outside of the lesson.

LINKED UNITS

- Some units are linked by topic or theme, or explore a particular skill at different levels. Opportunites for linking units are highlighted in the Planning Suggestion section of the lesson plan.

● How to use *Models for Writing*

A Models for Writing Unit

 **LESSON ONE**

 **LESSON TWO**

Model Text

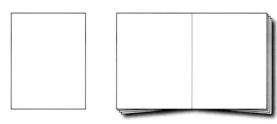

Overhead
Transparencies

Pupil's Book

Shared Writing

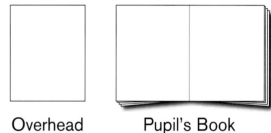

Overhead
Transparencies

Pupil's Book

Group Activities

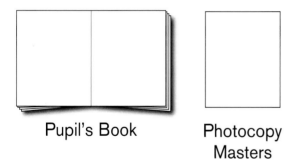

Pupil's Book

Photocopy
Masters

Guided/Supported Writing

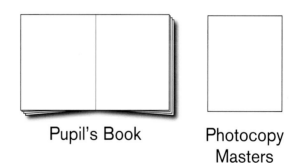

Pupil's Book

Photocopy
Masters

Homework

Photocopy
Masters

Extended Writing

Pupil's Book

How to use this *Teacher's Book*

main writing objective of unit with reference to NLS framework

unit number

unit heading

text type/ genre

word and sentence level objectives

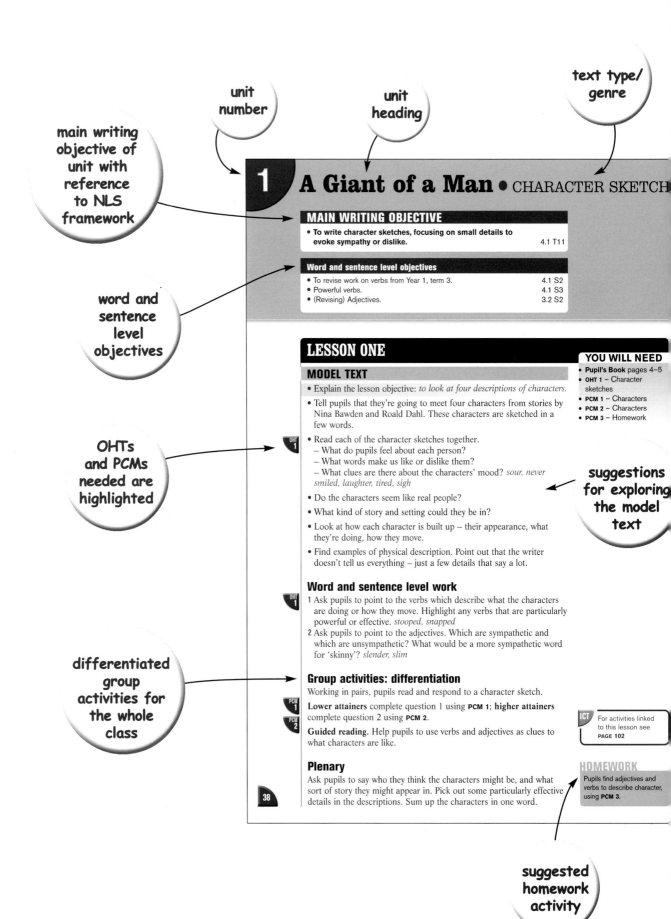

1 ## A Giant of a Man ● CHARACTER SKETCH

MAIN WRITING OBJECTIVE

● To write character sketches, focusing on small details to
evoke sympathy or dislike. 4.1 T11

Word and sentence level objectives

● To revise work on verbs from Year 1, term 3. 4.1 S2
● Powerful verbs. 4.1 S3
● (Revising) Adjectives. 3.2 S2

LESSON ONE

MODEL TEXT

● Explain the lesson objective: *to look at four descriptions of characters.*

● Tell pupils that they're going to meet four characters from stories by
Nina Bawden and Roald Dahl. These characters are sketched in a
few words.

● Read each of the character sketches together.
  – What do pupils feel about each person?
  – What words make us like or dislike them?
  – What clues are there about the characters' mood? *sour, never
  smiled, laughter, tired, sigh*

● Do the characters seem like real people?

● What kind of story and setting could they be in?

● Look at how each character is built up – their appearance, what
they're doing, how they move.

● Find examples of physical description. Point out that the writer
doesn't tell us everything – just a few details that say a lot.

Word and sentence level work

1 Ask pupils to point to the verbs which describe what the characters
are doing or how they move. Highlight any verbs that are particularly
powerful or effective. *stooped, snapped*
2 Ask pupils to point to the adjectives. Which are sympathetic and
which are unsympathetic? What would be a more sympathetic word
for 'skinny'? *slender, slim*

Group activities: differentiation
Working in pairs, pupils read and respond to a character sketch.

Lower attainers complete question 1 using **PCM 1**; **higher attainers**
complete question 2 using **PCM 2**.

Guided reading. Help pupils to use verbs and adjectives as clues to
what characters are like.

Plenary
Ask pupils to say who they think the characters might be, and what
sort of story they might appear in. Pick out some particularly effective
details in the descriptions. Sum up the characters in one word.

YOU WILL NEED
● **Pupil's Book** pages 4–5
● **OHT 1** – Character
sketches
● **PCM 1** – Characters
● **PCM 2** – Characters
● **PCM 3** – Homework

ICT For activities linked
to this lesson see
PAGE 102

HOMEWORK
Pupils find adjectives and
verbs to describe character,
using **PCM 3**.

OHTs and PCMs needed are highlighted

suggestions for exploring the model text

differentiated group activities for the whole class

suggested homework activity

38

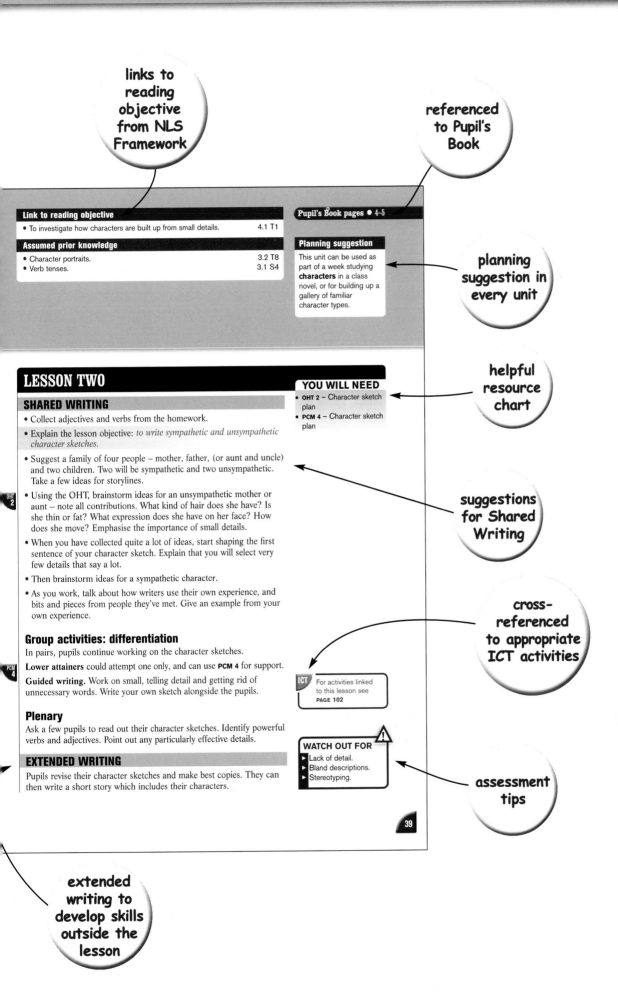

links to reading objective from NLS Framework

referenced to Pupil's Book

Link to reading objective
• To investigate how characters are built up from small details. 4.1 T1

Assumed prior knowledge
• Character portraits. 3.2 T8
• Verb tenses. 3.1 S4

Pupil's Book pages ● 4–5

Planning suggestion
This unit can be used as part of a week studying **characters** in a class novel, or for building up a gallery of familiar character types.

planning suggestion in every unit

helpful resource chart

LESSON TWO

SHARED WRITING
• Collect adjectives and verbs from the homework.
• Explain the lesson objective: *to write sympathetic and unsympathetic character sketches.*
• Suggest a family of four people – mother, father, (or aunt and uncle) and two children. Two will be sympathetic and two unsympathetic. Take a few ideas for storylines.
• Using the OHT, brainstorm ideas for an unsympathetic mother or aunt – note all contributions. What kind of hair does she have? Is she thin or fat? What expression does she have on her face? How does she move? Emphasise the importance of small details.
• When you have collected quite a lot of ideas, start shaping the first sentence of your character sketch. Explain that you will select very few details that say a lot.
• Then brainstorm ideas for a sympathetic character.
• As you work, talk about how writers use their own experience, and bits and pieces from people they've met. Give an example from your own experience.

Group activities: differentiation
In pairs, pupils continue working on the character sketches.
Lower attainers could attempt one only, and can use **PCM 4** for support.
Guided writing. Work on small, telling detail and getting rid of unnecessary words. Write your own sketch alongside the pupils.

Plenary
Ask a few pupils to read out their character sketches. Identify powerful verbs and adjectives. Point out any particularly effective details.

EXTENDED WRITING
Pupils revise their character sketches and make best copies. They can then write a short story which includes their characters.

YOU WILL NEED
• **OHT 2** – Character sketch plan
• **PCM 4** – Character sketch plan

OHT 2

PCM 4

suggestions for Shared Writing

cross-referenced to appropriate ICT activities

ICT For activities linked to this lesson see **PAGE 102**

⚠ **WATCH OUT FOR**
► Lack of detail.
► Bland descriptions.
► Stereotyping.

assessment tips

extended writing to develop skills outside the lesson

39

NLS Writing Objectives Matching Chart

MAIN WRITING OBJECTIVE	Unit 1 A Giant of a Man	Unit 2 Helping Each Other	Unit 3 The Magic Shoes	Unit 4 Fantastic Mr Fox	Unit 5 Feathers Fly!	Unit 6 The Evacuee	Unit 7 Up and Away!	Unit 8 Cats sleep fat	Unit 9 Young Archaeologist	Unit 10 A Wolf in Me	Unit 11 Weekend Bike Ride	Unit 12 The Iron Woman	Unit 13 How does it work?	Unit 14 The Emerald City of Oz	Unit 15 A Cautionary Tale	Unit 16 Robbers of the High Seas	Unit 17 Mr Creep the Crook	Unit 18 Talking to Rod Theodoru	Unit 19 Snake and Lizard	Unit 20 Red is like a trumpet sound	Unit 21 The Scrapyard of the Future	Unit 22 Jason and the School Bully 1	Unit 23 Jason and the School Bully 2	Unit 24 It's Not Fair!	Unit 25 It wasn't a brick…	Unit 26 Special Offer!	Unit 27 Childhood Tracks	Unit 28 I'm writing to ask	Unit 29 Skipping, Clapping and Counting	Unit 30 My Favourite Author
Term 1 – Fiction																														
4.1 T9 To use different ways of planning stories, e.g. brainstorming, notes, diagrams.		✓	✓																											
4.1 T10 To plan a story, identifying the stages of its telling.	✓																													
4.1 T11 To write character sketches, focusing on small details to evoke sympathy or dislike.				✓																										
4.1 T12 To write independently, linking own experience to situations in historical stories.						✓																								
4.1 T13 To write playscripts based on known stories.																														
4.1 T14 To write poems based on personal or imagined experience; experiment with powerful and expressive verbs.							✓			✓																				
4.1 T15 To use paragraphs in story writing to organise and sequence the narrative.								✓																						
Term 1 – Non-fiction																														
4.1 T24 To write a newspaper-style report, e.g. about school events or incidents from a story.					✓																									
4.1 T25 To write clear instructions using conventions learned from reading.											✓																			
4.1 T26 To improve the cohesion of written instructions and directions by using linking phrases and organisational devices.											✓																			
4.1 T27 To write a non-chronological report, including the use of organisational devices, e.g. numbered lists and headings.									✓																					
Term 2 – Fiction																														
4.2 T10 To develop use of settings, making use of work on adjectives and figurative language to describe them.														✓																
4.2 T11 To write poetry based on the structure and style of poems read, taking account of patterns of rhythm.															✓															
4.2 T12 To collaborate with others to write stories with particular audiences in mind.																	✓													
4.2 T13 To write descriptive, expressive language based on reading, linked to work on adjectives and similes.																			✓											
Term 2 – Non-fiction																														
4.2 T21 To make short notes, e.g. by abbreviating ideas, selecting key words, listing or in diagrammatic form.																✓		✓												
4.2 T22 To fill out brief notes into connected prose.																✓		✓												
4.2 T23 To collect information from a variety of sources and present it in one simple format.																				✓										
4.2 T24 To improve the cohesion of written explanations through paragraphing and the use of linking phrases and organisational devices.												✓	✓																	
4.2 T25 To write explanations of a process, using conventions identified through reading.													✓																	
Term 3 – Fiction																														
4.3 T11 To explore the main issue of a story by writing a story about a dilemma and the issues it raises for the character.																						✓								
4.3 T12 To write an alternative ending for a known story.																								✓						
4.3 T13 To write own longer stories in chapters from story plans.																					✓									
4.3 T14 To write poems, experimenting with different styles and structures.																											✓			
4.3 T15 To produce polished poetry through revision.																													✓	
Term 3 – Non-fiction																														
4.3 T21 To assemble and sequence points in order to plan the presentation of a point of view.																							✓		✓					
4.3 T22 To use writing frames to back up points of view with illustrations and examples.																										✓				✓
4.3 T23 To present a point of view in writing, e.g. in the form of a letter, linking points persuasively.																												✓		
4.3 T24 To summarise in writing the key ideas of a chapter or paragraph.																														

Scottish 5–14 Curriculum Guideline Levels

STRAND	LEVEL B	UNITS	LEVEL C	UNITS
Functional Writing	**Write briefly in an appropriate form for a variety of practical purposes.** • Letters and reports of events that they have been involved in • Simple notes to assist in sequencing events. • Consider audience – pupils, parents etc. • Write real letters to public figures, to seek information. • Teacher to introduce different styles of writing for different purposes.	5 30 9 11 13 16, 18 19	**Write in an appropriate form and with adequate vocabulary to communicate key events, facts or ideas.** • Use other contexts e.g. Env. Studies. • Purpose and audience should be established. • Note taking with teacher help – from TV etc with reports built from these. • Teacher help pupils analyse texts e.g. reading material to extract important data.	26 28
Personal Writing	**Write briefly and in an appropriate sequence about a personal experience, giving an indication of feelings, using adequate vocabulary.** • Sequence developed through pictures in order and a sentence written for each. • In discussion singly and in groups reflect on stories and reshape them. • Use other writing as models. • With teacher assistance begin to articulate feelings. • Use of concept keyboard.	8 10 20 24 27	**Write about a personal experience for a specific purpose and audience using appropriate organisation and vocabulary.** • The sense of purpose and audience will be developed for each type of writing. • Appropriate contexts used.	
Imaginative Writing	**Write a brief imaginative story or poem or dialogue with discernible organisation and using adequate vocabulary.** • Using a model and by discussing appropriate vocabulary teachers help pupils draft what they wish to say. • Discuss in groups first draft. • Teacher to introduce plot, character, setting, dialogue etc through class stories. • Model poetry through a wide variety of poems – rhyme less important than rhythm, content and vocabulary.	1 29 2 3 4 6 12 14 22 25	**Write a brief imaginative story, poem or play using appropriate organisation and vocabulary.** • Teacher will provide stimulating contexts for imaginative writing. • Teacher draw attention to character, scene, setting and action. • Pupils begin to look at events from the point of view of different characters. • Poetry developed to include reading aloud own and others' work.	7 15 17 23
Punctuation and Structure	**In the writing tasks listed use capital letters and full stops correctly in more than one sentence and use common linking words – and then, but, so, that.** • Use capital letters and full stops to establish meaning through teacher support. • Link sentences with common and familiar words.	4 29 13 16 21 24 27	**In the writing tasks listed punctuate many sentences accurately including simple use of commas and question marks; begin to use paragraphs to structure writing.** • Teacher still models use of the above and encourages pupils to use them in own writing. • Co-operative writing can be used to aid group discussion and reinforce sense of audience and motivate re-drafting skills.	5 7 8, 9 22 23 25
Knowledge About Language	**Show that they know understand and can use at least the following terms – letter, word, capital letter, full stop, sentence, planning, drafting, editing.** • Teacher to model all of these in reading etc and pupils should be aware of them in their own work. • Pupils will use planning drafting and editing throughout the writing process.	1 17 2 18 3 19 10 20 11 26 12 28 14 30 15	**Show that they know understand and can use at least the following terms – noun, verb, comma, question mark, purpose, audience.** • Teacher will continue to model these through class novels etc and encourage pupils to ensure they use all these conventions in their own work.	5 6 7 8 9

The strands for Spelling and Handwriting and Presentation would be covered by the teacher differentiating according to each pupil's ability.

Models for Writing and the Northern Ireland Curriculum

UNIT	LEVEL	Opportunities are provided for:
1	3/4	
2	3/4	**WRITING**
3	4	• Modelled writing
4	4	• Shared writing
5	4	• Writing for a variety of purposes and audiences
6	4	• Planning, drafting, revising, and publishing • Collaborative work
7	4	• Children to see their teacher write • Extending vocabulary
8	3/4	• Using appropriate form, showing a sense of structure and organisation
9	4	• Discussing features of layout • Gathering and organising ideas
10	4	• Using some supporting detail to improve meaning
11	3/4	• Presenting ideas and information logically • Developing knowledge of and using basic punctuation with accuracy
12	4	• Responding to reading
13	4	• Teaching note making • Using problem solving to analyse texts
14	4	• Experimenting with rhymes, rhythms, verbal play and poetic forms
15	3/4	• Differentiated responses
16	4	**READING**
17	4	• Reading aloud
18	4	• Using a range of vocabulary when referring to texts • Composing, reading and sharing their own books of stories and poems
19	3/4	• Modelling writing on forms encountered in reading • Recognising the main points
20	4	• Recognising a sequence of events
21	3/4	• Using evidence in the text to support their views • Talking about the features of written language
22	4	• Reading for a variety of purposes
23	4	• Recognising and expressing explicit and some implicit meanings in a range of texts
24	4	• Supporting a response with reference to text
25	3/4	• Becoming aware of the writer's intentions and use of language and structure
26	4	• Shared reading • Modelled reading
27	4	• Independent reading
28	4	• Engaging with a range of texts
29	3/4	**TALKING AND LISTENING**
30	3/4	• Engaging in formal and informal discussion
		• Giving instructions, information and explanations
		• Talking about their work to other pupils and the teacher
		• Expressing thoughts, feelings and opinions
		• Listening to and saying poems
		• Listening to and responding to guidance and instructions given by the teacher
		• Describing and talking about real and imagined experiences
		• Sharing and co-operating in pairs and small groups
		• Discussing features of language

●About Shared Writing

In Shared Writing, you, the 'expert writer', model the writing process. Pupils should contribute ideas, calling on their experience of exploring the model text, and you develop them further.

Before Writing

Talk with the pupils about:

- the text type and its features ●
- the purpose and audience ●
- the structure, and how best to order the events or information
- the layout – length, illustration and final presentation
- possible ways of planning – brainstorming, story boards, writing ● frames etc.

What do we know about texts like these?

Who are we writing for?

How can we organise our ideas?

During Shared Writing

- where appropriate, display the annotated model text so the class can refer to it
- explain exactly what you like or do not like about the ideas the pupils offer
- demonstrate how to share ideas and work collaboratively
- 'think aloud' as you write so that pupils understand how to ● consider different options
- demonstrate how writers work at each stage of composition
- show pupils how to apply the conventions of written English – focus on specific aspects of punctuation or spelling
- demonstrate how to revise the writing by re-reading and making changes
- keep the writing short.

I'm making this into a longer sentence by adding extra detail.

After Writing

Show pupils how to:

- talk about their writing; introduce the vocabulary they will need
- edit and redraft their work, perhaps moving larger chunks of text ● as well as adding and deleting words and phrases
- make the link again between reading and writing, considering their work as a reader would – What does it make you feel? What is left ● out or not clear?
- proof-read, checking for sense as well as spelling and punctuation errors
- prepare for final presentation.

Let's add an adjective to describe what he looks like. How should we describe him?

Does this sound right? Is it better if we take out these words?

REMEMBER

Do

- share the lesson objective with the pupils
- emphasise purpose and audience
- refer back to the model text
- direct and control the Shared Writing
- encourage pupils to contribute at their own level
- build on pupils' suggestions
- write with pupils whenever possible
- 'think aloud' as you are writing
- encourage pupils to revise as they write
- teach self-help techniques
- expect pupils to proof-read and edit their work

Don't

- offer unfocused praise
- be afraid to make specific criticisms
- try to correct every aspect of their writing

About Guided Writing

Guided Writing is about providing support for children during the writing process.

For Guided Writing, children should be in small groups according to writing ability. You may teach specific skills, or dip in and out of writing with the pupils, discussing as you go. Providing support while children are working is especially important.

Offer guidance throughout the writing process. On pages 16–19 you will find Prompt Charts to help you guide pupils through each stage of composition.

Before Writing

Help pupils to prepare by:

- reviewing the task ●

Who are we writing for?

- collecting ideas – maybe by brainstorming or spider webbing
- talking about how to organise the material – choosing key ideas, grouping them, putting them in the best order, working out how to link them

How shall we group all our ideas?

- jotting down words and phrases that might be useful
- checking for gaps in their plan.

During Writing

Join the group when they are already writing. Observe for a while, then:

- find out how it is going and identify any problems
- focus on specific elements of composition, just a few sentences at a ● time

What could we add to give us more detail?

- remind pupils of the model text and the work done in Shared Writing
- help to develop ideas and build confidence ●
- use appropriate terminology.

That's a really good connective because...

After Writing

Respond to pupils' work by:

- finding out what the writers were trying to achieve ●

What are we looking for in this text?

- reviewing the task and recapping the features of the text type
- asking writers to read out sections they are pleased with
- giving precise, positive feedback which lets writers know what effect ● their writing has had on a reader

I liked the bit when...

- asking writers to identify the parts which need development
- encouraging suggestions for improvement.

Teaching sequence for Guided Writing when planning written work

STEPS	TYPICAL CUES
Review	• What do we know about writing texts like this? • What is the job in hand? • How shall we go about it?
Gather ideas	• What do we want to say? • What ideas do we have?
Marshal the material (select – shape – sequence)	• Which ideas shall we use? • How can we group ideas together? • What order should we put them in? • How can we link the ideas together?
Gather support	• What details can we add? • How can we explain or expand? • What evidence can we give? • What words and expressions come to mind?
Rehearse	• Does it look right? • What are the gaps? • How could we start? • How can it be improved?

Teaching sequence for Guided Writing when pupils are drafting

STEPS	TYPICAL CUES
Review	• What's the task in hand? • What do we know already? • What are the main features of this kind of text? • How did the author in yesterday's Shared Reading tackle this?
Cue in	• How might you start? • Let me start you off . . . • Let's try starting with action this time.
Try it	• Identification • Exploration/generalisation • Addition/deletion/substitution • Praise/building confidence • Assessment • Use of terminology/reflection • Extension/development • Drawing writing into talk
Recapitulate	• What worked? • What helped? • What can we use again?

Teaching sequence for Guided Writing when responding to written work

STEPS	TYPICAL CUES
Recapitulate	• What are we looking for in this piece of writing? • What are the main features of this kind of text?
Read and reward	• What I liked about this was . . . • That makes me wonder . . . • I noticed . . . • Where are the best moments?
Compare and generalise	• Who else tried it that way? • What other ways have been used? • Which of these worked well? • Which tends to work best?
Isolate weakness	• Where are the false notes? • Why does it not quite work? • Which is the hardest part to get right? • What could be improved?
Support improvement	• How could you deal with the problem? • Could we say . . .? • You could try . . . • Start like this . . . • Try writing that part again . . .

Teaching activities: intervening in the writing process

1 Identification/Selection of important features	What I noticed/liked about this was . . . because . . .
2 Addition Deletion Substitution	What can we add? What can we leave out/get rid of? What else can we put in there to make it better?
3 Exploration/Generalisation	The reason why . . . It's useful to know that . . . What tends to work best is . . . because . . . The rule/pattern for this is . . . When else does this happen?
4 Praise/Building confidence	I really like the way you . . . because . . . I really like . . . because . . . That works well because . . .
5 Assessment Assessing strengths, weaknesses Correction	Which parts work best? Why does it not quite work? Which is the hardest part to get right?
6 Use of terminology/Reflection	I really like the term you chose because . . . Which term could you use here?
7 Extension/Development	Could we use, say . . .? You could try . . . You can carry on by . . .
8 Drawing writing into talking	Tell me how you would write . . . So you think that . . . What do you think about . . .? Say a little more about . . .

Independent and Extended Writing

Independent Writing

Independent writing activities flow directly from Shared or Guided Writing. In independent group activities, pupils are still supported by working collaboratively and by using writing frames. **Writing frames can be a powerful support for writers but they can also become a straightjacket. It is very important to show pupils how to adapt them and how to generate their own.** Support also comes from exploring the model text, the preparatory work completed for homework and the Shared Writing session.

Models for Writing also provides **Prompt Charts** which list the main features of each text type or writing process, and these can be displayed for pupils to refer to. (The **Prompt Charts** are located at the back of the **Photocopy Masters** folder.)

Extended Writing

The suggestions for extended writing in *Models for Writing* encourage pupils to carry on with their writing outside the Literacy Hour; to discuss and revise their work; to take their work to presentation standard and, where appropriate, to publish it using ICT. The lesson plans that accompany each unit offer suggestions for how you might integrate the units and the extended writing activities into your weekly planning.

Models for Writing emphasises that writing for different purposes requires different approaches. A shopping list or a quick note will not require redrafting, but a brochure about the school, or a web site, might take several sessions to complete.

Pair and Collaborative Writing: Response Partners

Models for Writing offers pupils ample opportunity to talk about their work and to help each other by giving feedback, as well as times when they can write in near silence. Their feedback will be most effective if they are given guidance and practice in reading each other's work and giving advice on it. Encourage them to act as response partners on a regular basis.

At first their comments may be superficial. They need to learn to:

- find out what the writer is trying to do
- pay attention to content
- identify which features to comment on
- balance positive and negative comments
- be constructive.

On pages 32–34 you will find **Self-Assessment** sheets to support this process. Discuss and model the process in Shared and Guided Writing.

Knowing it is good or bad is not good enough!

To reach literacy targets, we need to know *precisely* what pupils need to improve upon. What are the features in pupil X's writing that make him so fluent? What *exactly* are the difficulties that pupil Y is having which may prevent her reaching level 4 by the end of Key Stage 2? If you can diagnose the symptoms you are on the way to finding a cure. Through careful assessment and specific feedback, you and your pupils will find out what they can do already and what they need to do next. On the basis of this you can plan future tasks to take their learning forward. The most helpful assessments focus on a few specific features. Too much information can be overwhelming and de-motivating.

If the learning objective is clear and precise then assessment is easy. Much of the assessment occurs with the pupil during writing, particularly in guided group work. Talking together helps you to find out what the writer is trying to do and what difficulties they are encountering.

Pupils can also get feedback for themselves. Make sure they know the purpose of every writing task and the criteria for assessing it. Show them how to assess their own writing against the criteria and how to work effectively with a response partner.

Prompt Charts

To check whether the piece of writing has the appropriate structure and features for its 'genre' or 'text type', use the Prompt Charts at the back of the **Photocopy Masters** folder.

You can also give these charts to pupils to help them remember the criteria, and structure their writing accordingly.

Self-Assessment

Ask pupils to use **Photocopy Master** A (*see page 32*) to assist their work with a response partner. They can also use **Photocopy Master** B (*see page 33*) to support their editing, and **Photocopy Master** C (*see page 34*) to assess their own work.

Help them to develop the habit of reflecting on their own writing. If they are involved in setting their own targets they will be much more motivated to achieve them.

Questions to Consider

Purpose and audience

- Is the form of the writing suitable for its purpose?
- Is the writer aware of the reader?
- Does the writing engage the reader's interest?

Structure and organisation

- How effective are the opening and ending?
- How well does the writer organise ideas?
- Does the structure reflect the features of the text type?
- Is sentence construction varied?
- Are sentences and paragraphs joined with a variety of connectives?

Grammar and style

- Is the writing grammatically correct?
- Is punctuation used correctly?
- Are verb tenses consistent?
- Is there unnecessary repetition?
- Does the writing flow?
- Is it coherent?
- Is the vocabulary well chosen?

Presentation

- Is handwriting or word processing clear and suitable for the purpose?
- Is the presentation appropriate?

Spelling

- Is spelling usually accurate?
- Does spelling show knowledge of word derivation, common patterns, and prefixes/suffixes?
- Are guesses plausible?

Fiction: The Room
Achievements: Level 4
Purpose and audience
NLS 4.2 T10 To develop the use of settings in own writing.

Summary

The exercise was part of a follow-up from a workshop with a visiting writer. Joshua has a good grasp of the task set – to describe a setting which reflects the main character, for the opening of a story. He shows awareness of the reader and is skilled in engaging their interest. He is also conscious of the effect of a final sentence.

Structure and Organisation

- Confident, controlled construction.
- Carefully planted clues (e.g. two mugs) to build up a picture of the character.
- Well selected, telling detail.
- Some variation in sentence construction.

Grammar and Style

- Shows literary influence in writing, e.g. 'ready for a pencil's touch'; 'On the desk was. . .'.
- Precise vocabulary – toppling, gentle, smell.
- Strong sense of atmosphere.
- No apostrophes or speech marks.

Spelling

- Very competent spelling.
- Good grasp of irregular phonemes – straight, touch, minute – and -le and -ing endings.

What next?

- Continue the piece by writing an extended story in chapters.
- Investigate descriptions of setting in examples of more challenging literature.
- Reinforce rules for speech marks.

The Room

The walls were full of used books.

On the desk was a note pad ready for a pencils touch, and next to it was two empty coffee mugs. The computer was left on with an unfinished poem on it. There was a gentle smell of pencil lead. The bin was toppling over with lots of different sorts of paper screwed up in it. The chair was very simple and had a dead straight back. The clock was five minutes early. There was a note on the desk saying gone out back in a few hours. That room was silent.

by Joshua King

Writing Sample 2: Level 3/4 Fiction

Fiction: Flat Stanley Newspaper Report
Achievements: Level 3, with some elements of Level 4
Purpose and audience:
NLS 4.1 T24 To write newspaper style reports, composing headlines, using IT to draft and lay out; editing stories to fit particular space; organising writing into paragraphs.

Summary
This piece was done in response to a class novel. The writer shows an awareness of audience, and engages the reader with a chatty style. The piece shows good knowledge of the text type.

Structure and Organisation
• Competent, economical summary of plot showing good knowledge of characters and events.

• Effective headline and use of journalistic features, e.g. rhetorical questions, quoting from interviews etc.

Grammar and Style
• Vocabulary well chosen to reflect text type – racy, chatty style; alliteration.

• Use of present and past tense accurate and consistent.

• Speech marks accurate, but no paragraphs.

Spelling
• Carefully corrected using a spellchecker.

What next?
• More work on paragraphs – study their use in a tabloid newspaper.

• Compose captions and sub-headings.

• Give him challenging poetry to read and discuss.

A FLAT PROBLEM

MR AND MRS LAMBCHOP HAVE A FLAT PROBLEM. THEIR SON STANLEY IS A CENTIMETRE THICK. HE CAN SLIDE UNDER DOORS. HIS BROTHER WANTED TO FLY A KITE. WHAT DID STANLEY DO? GET SOME STRING AND BE ONE. HE SAVED HIS MUMS RING FROM DOWN THE DRAIN. NOW WE HEAR WHAT THE FLAT FLYING FOLK HAS TO SAY. "I WAS SLEEPING LAST NIGHT WHEN MY PIN BOARD FELL ON TOP OF ME, AND WHEN MY BROTHER WOKE ME UP I WAS LIKE THIS. BUT I FEEL O.K NOW" WELL SAID MY -BOY. NOW LETS HEAR FROM DOCTOR DAN "I DONT THINK I'VE SEEN ANYTHING LIKE IT -YOU ARE, READ NEXT TIME. THATS ALL FOLKS.

DRINK MORE GUINESS BEER

27

Non-Fiction: Toffee Machine
Achievements: Level 3, with some elements of Level 4
Purpose and audience:
NLS 4.2 T25 To write explanations of a process.

Summary

The writer shows a good understanding of the task set, which was to invent/design a machine and to explain how it works, using diagrams.

Structure and Organisation

- Some features of explanatory texts have been well grasped: present tense, time connectives (when, then), sequential explanation, cause and effect.

- Lacks a clear introduction describing the machine's purpose.

Grammar and Style

- Competent, coherent style.

- Consistent verbs, apart from 'freezed'.

- No paragraphs.

Spelling

- Good grasp of conventions.

- Most polysyllabic words correctly spelt.

What next?

- Investigate the use of numbered bullet points and similar devices in explanatory texts.

- Discuss where other paragraph breaks should be.

Toffee chocolate bonbon machine

You put sugar, syrup and margarine into its own container. and then it mixes up in the toffee mixer to make toffee. When it is ready it goes down to the ice department to solidifie the toffee. Then you put cocaa, milk and sugar in it own compartment and mixes into chocdate and get freezed over the toffee. Then it gets wrapped up in the wrapping machine.

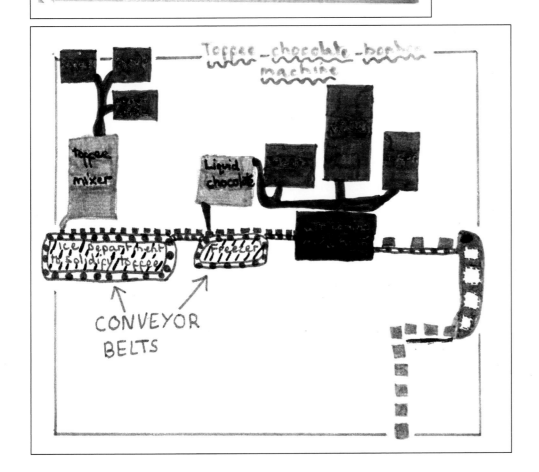

Toffee chocolate bonbon machine

toffee mixer

Liquid chocolate

Ice department to solidify toffee

Freezer

CONVEYOR BELTS

Non-fiction: Advertisement
Achievements: Level 3
Purpose and audience:
NLS 4.3 T25 To design an advertisement.

Summary

The writing was linked to work in Design and Technology – to design and promote a new product. The chosen form is suitable for the purpose (the original was A3 and in colour). The writer shows awareness of persuasive language devices, and successfully grabs the reader's attention. The piece also displays awareness of layout requirements, with the use of bubbles, and different styles and sizes of font, but it is poorly presented for a final copy.

Structure and Organisation

- Good use of alliteration.

- Use of typical exaggerated claims – 'You'll never believe. . .'

- Essential information is appropriately conveyed.

- Uses a variety of sentence construction.

Grammar and Style

- Correct use of passive verbs – 'to be won' – and imperative verbs – 'always check'.

- Well chosen vocabulary.

- Punchy style.

- Bottom bubble unpunctuated.

Spelling

- Erratic but generally plausible.

- Occasional careless slips.

What next?

- Discuss strategies for self-checking spelling errors.

- Work on lower-case print for special design purposes.

- Look at examples of layout, using magazines etc to cut up and arrange print.

TRY OUR NEW
Cadburys
MONSTER MUNCH CHOCLATE CHIP-COOKIES
You'll Never Belive The Price 25p Packet
Made with Didesti Biscuits
MMM
I'M Coming for you Monster
Monster choclat chip Shap.
I'M a COOKIE Eat Me!
Monster Munch Choclat Chip-COOKIES
Allways check your packet thereor some lovely prizes to be won there is a bonus prize a £1.0000 Pound Ferrari F50

Working with a response partner

Read your work aloud.

Is it interesting/enjoyable?

Is anything not clear? List below.

●

●

●

Is anything missing? List below.

●

●

●

Can you suggest:

● alternative words or expressions?

● a better beginning or ending?

Is it too long or too short?

Can anything be cut? If so, what?

Has the writer done what he or she was asked to do?

Remember to check:	checked ✓
Are there enough details to help the reader?	☐
Have you used capital letters and punctuation?	☐
Is speech set out correctly?	☐
Do all verbs and nouns agree?	☐
Are all spellings correct?	☐
Are there any repeated phrases or unneccessary words that you can take out?	☐

Self-assessment

Title of writing: _____

What was the task? _____

_____

_____

How difficult was it? (Circle the score out of 10)

    1   2   3   4   5   6   7   8   9   10

How happy are you with it? (Circle the score out of 10)

    1   2   3   4   5   6   7   8   9   10

What do you think you have done well?

_____

_____

What didn't work?

_____

_____

What did your response partner say about it?

_____

_____

Do you agree?

_____

What is your new target?

_____

_____

Models for Writing and SATs preparation

The six pieces of writing below can be set under timed conditions. It is a good idea to set one piece of timed writing every half term. Give the pupils 15 minutes to plan the task and 45 minutes to complete their writing.

Unit 5 Feathers Fly!

TASK: Write a newspaper report about a real event, or an event from a story.

Assessment Criteria

Purpose and audience

- Is the form of writing suitable for the purpose and audience?
- Does the writing engage the reader?
- Is there a good use of journalistic features?
- Does the article include facts, opinions and quotes?
- Is the layout appropriate?

Grammar and style

- Does the choice of vocabulary reflect the text type?
- Is the use of present and past tense accurate and consistent?
- Are speech marks used accurately?
- Are paragraphs used correctly?

Unit 6 The Evacuee

TASK: Write a story in which you are an evacuee. Include a description of how you felt and what you did.

Assessment Criteria

Purpose and audience

- Is the form of writing suitable for the purpose and audience?
- Are events well ordered in logical sequence?
- Does the writer engage the reader's interest?
- How effective are the opening and ending?
- Are a variety of connectives used?

Grammar and style

- Is the story written in the first person?
- Does the writing include how the author feels, what s/he does, what s/he says?
- Is dialogue used?
- Are sentence correctly indicated by full stops, capital letters and question marks?

Unit 13 How does it work?

TASK: Write an explanation of how a simple machine works. Make
sure the drawing/diagram is clearly labelled.

Assessment Criteria

Purpose and audience

- Is the form of writing suitable for its purpose?
- Is the writer aware of the reader?
- Is the writing organised into logically sequenced short
  paragraphs?
- Is there a short introductory statement?
- Has thought been given to layout and use of diagrams?

Grammar and style

- Is it written in the present tense?
- Are causal connectives used?
- Does it use impersonal language?
- Is the explanation coherent?
- Is the vocabulary well chosen?

Unit 19 Snake and Lizard

TASK: Write a Fact File about your favourite animal.

Assessment Criteria

Purpose and audience

- Is the form of writing suitable for its purpose?
- Is the writer aware of the reader?
- Does the writer use short sentences?
- Is the writing organised in a coherent way?
- Has thought been given to the layout and use of captions?

Grammar and style

- Is the vocabulary well chosen?
- Is it written in the present tense?
- Are the sentences correctly punctuated?

Unit 24 It's Not Fair!

TASK: Write an argument on a subject that you think is not fair.

Assessment Criteria

Purpose and audience

- Is the form of writing suitable for its purpose?
- Is the writer aware of the reader?
- How effectively is the debate introduced?
- Is the argument effectively structured, showing both points of view?
- How well is the writer's opinion organised?

Grammar and style

- Are sentences correctly indicted by full stops, capital letters and question marks?
- Is the chosen vocabulary appropriate?
- Is the argument organised into paragraphs?
- Is the writing coherent?

Unit 26 Special Offer!

TASK: Design an advertisement for a product of your choice.

Assessment Criteria

Purpose and audience

- Is the form of writing suitable for its purpose?
- Is there a variety of sentence construction?
- Does the advert contain special offers and exaggerated claims?
- Is the writer aware of the reader?
- Is the layout appropriate?

Grammar and style

- Is the vocabulary well chosen?
- Is the style of the writing appropriate?
- Is the writing grammatically correct?
- Is punctuation used correctly?
- Is the writing persuasive?

MAIN WRITING OBJECTIVE

- **To write character sketches, focusing on small details to
  evoke sympathy or dislike.**   4.1 T11

Word and sentence level objectives

- To revise work on verbs from Year 1, term 3.   4.1 S2
- Powerful verbs.   4.1 S3
- (Revising) Adjectives.   3.2 S2

LESSON ONE

MODEL TEXT

- Explain the lesson objective: *to look at four descriptions of characters.*

- Tell pupils that they're going to meet four characters from stories by
  Nina Bawden and Roald Dahl. These characters are sketched in a
  few words.

- Read each of the character sketches together.
  – What do pupils feel about each person?
  – What words make us like or dislike them?
  – What clues are there about the characters' mood? *sour, never
  smiled, laughter, tired, sigh*

- Do the characters seem like real people?

- What kind of story and setting could they be in?

- Look at how each character is built up – their appearance, what
  they're doing, how they move.

- Find examples of physical description. Point out that the writer
  doesn't tell us everything – just a few details that say a lot.

Word and sentence level work

1 Ask pupils to point to the verbs which describe what the characters
  are doing or how they move. Highlight any verbs that are particularly
  powerful or effective. *stooped, snapped*
2 Ask pupils to point to the adjectives. Which are sympathetic and
  which are unsympathetic? What would be a more sympathetic word
  for 'skinny'? *slender, slim*

Group activities: differentiation

Working in pairs, pupils read and respond to a character sketch.

Lower attainers complete question 1 using **PCM 1**; **higher attainers**
complete question 2 using **PCM 2**.

Guided reading. Help pupils to use verbs and adjectives as clues to
what characters are like.

Plenary

Ask pupils to say who they think the characters might be, and what
sort of story they might appear in. Pick out some particularly effective
details in the descriptions. Sum up the characters in one word.

YOU WILL NEED

- **Pupil's Book** pages 4–5
- **OHT 1** – Character
  sketches
- **PCM 1** – Characters
- **PCM 2** – Characters
- **PCM 3** – Homework

 ICT For activities linked
to this lesson see
PAGE 102

HOMEWORK

Pupils find adjectives and
verbs to describe character,
using **PCM 3**.

Pupil's Book pages ● 4–5

Planning suggestion

This unit can be used as part of a week studying **characters** in a class novel, or for building up a gallery of familiar character types.

LESSON TWO

SHARED WRITING

• Collect adjectives and verbs from the homework.

• Explain the lesson objective: *to write sympathetic and unsympathetic character sketches.*

• Suggest a family of four people – mother, father, (or aunt and uncle) and two children. Two will be sympathetic and two unsympathetic. Take a few ideas for storylines.

• Using the OHT, brainstorm ideas for an unsympathetic mother or aunt – note all contributions. What kind of hair does she have? Is she thin or fat? What expression does she have on her face? How does she move? Emphasise the importance of small details.

• When you have collected quite a lot of ideas, start shaping the first sentence of your character sketch. Explain that you will select very few details that say a lot.

• Then brainstorm ideas for a sympathetic character.

• As you work, talk about how writers use their own experience, and bits and pieces from people they've met. Give an example from your own experience.

Group activities: differentiation

In pairs, pupils continue working on the character sketches.

Lower attainers could attempt one only, and can use **PCM 4** for support.

Guided writing. Work on small, telling detail and getting rid of unnecessary words. Write your own sketch alongside the pupils.

Plenary

Ask a few pupils to read out their character sketches. Identify powerful verbs and adjectives. Point out any particularly effective details.

EXTENDED WRITING

Pupils revise their character sketches and make best copies. They can then write a short story which includes their characters.

YOU WILL NEED

• **OHT 2** – Character sketch plan
• **PCM 4** – Character sketch plan

ICT For activities linked to this lesson see **PAGE 102**

WATCH OUT FOR

▶ Lack of detail.
▶ Bland descriptions.
▶ Stereotyping.

Helping Each Other

● RESPONSE PARTNERS

MAIN WRITING OBJECTIVE

- **The main objective of this unit is to discuss attitudes to writing and methods of support.**

Other objectives

- To use different ways of planning. — 4.1 T9
- To write instructions. — 4.1 T25

LESSON ONE

WHOLE CLASS

- Explain the lesson objective: *to explore the sort of feedback that helps us most with our writing.*

- Encourage a general discussion about what the pupils find helpful and unhelpful. Talk about how writers can help each other by working together. Nobody likes changing their work when it's finished. It's much easier to revise as you go along. **Emphasise that response partners can help each other at any stage from planning to final presentation.**

- Read together what some other children said about working with a response partner: **How helpful is my partner?** Do pupils agree or disagree with the comments?

- Now make notes on the OHT as you discuss how a response partner can help with pupils' writing. Ask pupils how they think they can help each other before writing. *give each other ideas, brainstorm together, look at each other's plans*

- How do they think they can help each other during writing? *reading bits out to see if they sound right, suggesting words to use*

- How can they help each other after writing? *suggesting revisions*

Group activities: differentiation

Pupils work in pairs to read and discuss the questionnaire on **PCM 5**. They can then start to fill it in. Before they start, make sure they understand the terms planning and drafting.

Plenary

1 Compare views on the questionnaire. What makes pupils do a really good piece of writing?

2 Ask pupils what else helps them to make their work better and makes them enjoy writing. *they may say if their parents will see it, or if it's to go on the wall*

3 Look briefly at the comments in the Pupil's Book under **What is my writing for?** Explain that we all write better when we know who our audience is (who we are writing for) and the purpose of our writing (why and what we are writing). Our partners can help us to think about these things.

YOU WILL NEED

- **Pupil's Book** pages 6–7
- **OHT 3** – Before, During and After
- **PCM 5** – Questionnaire

 ICT For activities linked to this lesson see **PAGE 102**

HOMEWORK

Pupils ask parents or other adults what types of writing they do and what they find easy and difficult. Ask them what they remember about writing when they were at school.

Assumed prior knowledge

- Basic understanding of the writing process – planning, drafting, revising, editing and publishing.
- Some practice of keeping spelling logs during Year 3.
- Experience of working with a response partner.
- Instructions.

3.2 T16

Pupil's Book pages ● 6–7

Planning suggestion

This unit links to Unit 3 to form a whole week's work. The focus of this unit is to discuss how pupils can help each other in all stages of the writing process. In the following unit they will work through the writing process using the techniques they have learned here.

LESSON TWO

SHARED WRITING

- Spend a few minutes discussing the homework.

- Explain the lesson objective: *to write tips for response partners.*

- Remind pupils of yesterday's discussion and of the tips for response partners in the Pupil's Book. When can a response partner help? In what way? What responses are not helpful?

- Can pupils think of any more tips?

- Demonstrate brainstorming – calling out words, phrases and ideas in any order, without commenting on others' ideas.

- Scribe for a few minutes on the flipchart but don't exhaust all the ideas. Explain that they'll be brainstorming some more during group work.

- Discuss how you might structure the tips. Look at the ideas and see if they could be grouped together under the headings: Before, During and After.

- Show pupils how to group the ideas by circling or underlining with the same colour.

- Then write out one or two tips under one of the headings. Write in the form of a simple instruction. Begin the sentence with an imperative verb. Quickly remind them of the features of instructions.

Group activities: differentiation

In pairs, pupils brainstorm and continue to plan 'Tips for response partners', using **PCM 6** for support. **Lower attainers** can simply list five tips, instead of using the 'Before, During and After' structure.

Guided writing. Offer guidance on organising ideas. Ask pupils how they are going to present their instructions. Discuss features such as bullet points or numbered lists and possible formats – booklet, poster, etc.

Plenary

Ask pupils to report on their work in progress. Continue to discuss ideas for presentation.

EXTENDED WRITING

Pupils continue writing and revising their tips, then make the final version into a booklet or poster which they can refer to throughout the year.

YOU WILL NEED

- **Pupil's Book** pages 6–7
- **PCM 6** – Before, During and After
- Flipchart

 For activities linked to this lesson see **PAGE 102**

WATCH OUT FOR

▶ Difficulty in remembering instructional language and features.
▶ Lack of structure.

41

MAIN WRITING OBJECTIVES

- To use different ways of planning stories, e.g brainstorming, notes, diagrams.   4.1 T9
- To plan a story, identifying the stages of its telling.   4.1 T10

Word and sentence level objective

- To revise work on verb tenses; to develop awareness of how verb tense relates to the structure and purpose of a text. e.g. narrative in past tense.   4.1 S2

LESSON ONE

MODEL TEXT

- Explain the lesson objective: *to read a story by a Year 4 pupil, and then look at where he got his ideas and how he planned his writing.*

- Read aloud the first paragraph of John's story. Ask pupils what sort of story they think this is this going to be.

- Read the rest of the story. With pupils, identify the main stages of the story – Introduction and Build-up: Paul finds the shoes; Climax: three wishes; Resolution: Paul wishes the genie away and things go back to normal.

- Look at the opening of the story. Stories often begin with 'One day . . .'. What has John added? Why? *one normal day – so that the appearance of the genie is even more surprising*

OHT 4 • Explain that John got the ideas for his story by looking at a pair of old shoes. Look at John's spider diagram together and talk about how he brainstormed his ideas, before going on to plan his story.

- Produce the objects and choose one to work with. Spend a few minutes brainstorming ideas. Where did it come from? What was it used for? Who does it belong to? What might be special about it? Note down the ideas.

Word and sentence level work

PB Ask pupils to pick out some of the verbs in John's story. What tense are they? Explain that stories are usually written in the past tense because the events have already happened.

Group activities: differentiation

Pupils work in groups to brainstorm story ideas based on the objects on their table. Choose one pupil to scribe a spider diagram of all their ideas. Remind pupils about helping each other to come up with good ideas. Display the **Prompt Chart**.

Give a **lower attaining** group the object from the shared session.

Guided group. Help pupils to go beyond their first ideas and come up with more adventurous possibilities. Get them asking questions.

Plenary

Ask pupils to share their ideas for a story. Which ideas do they like and why?

YOU WILL NEED

- **Pupil's Book** pages 8–9
- **OHT 4** – John's spider diagram
- A variety of objects, one for each group, to inspire ideas for stories.
- **Prompt Chart 1** – Response partner rules
- Flipchart

 ICT For activities linked to this lesson see **PAGE 102**

HOMEWORK

Ask pupils to brainstorm more ideas for the object they were looking at in group work and to make their own spider diagram.

Link to reading objective

- To explore narrative order and map out the main stages of a story. 4.1 T4

Assumed prior knowledge

- Response partner work and tips from Unit 2.
- Basic understanding of story writing process – planning, drafting, revising, editing, publishing.
- To plan the main points as a structure for story writing. 3.2 T6

Pupil's Book pages ● 8–9

Planning suggestion

This unit follows on from Unit 2, as part of a week looking at using a response partner throughout the writing process of planning, drafting, revising, editing and publishing. Pupils use the tips they wrote in Unit 2 to help each other plan and write a story.

LESSON TWO

SHARED WRITING

- Explain the lesson objective: *to plan a story using the ideas generated on a spider diagram.*

- Display the enlarged copy of one of the spider diagrams from yesterday's group work. Ask pupils to add some more ideas.

- Explain that you are going to plan a story based on these ideas. Show pupils how to underline the ideas they are going to use.

- Begin to plan the story together on the flipchart. Plot the main stages, showing pupils how to make notes.
  - How should the story begin?
  - What will happen? How will you build up the story? What will the climax be?
  - How will the story end? Make sure it doesn't just tail off.

- When you are finished, go back over the plan. Does the beginning still make sense? Can you tie it to the ending? Are there any other details you could add?

- Model writing an opening paragraph. Remind them about introducing character and setting the scene.

Group activities: differentiation

All pupils plan their own story using the ideas from their group brainstorm, or from homework. **PCM 7** is provided for support. They should swap their plans with a response partner and comment using the tips from Unit 2.

Guided writing. Make sure pupils' plans have a clear structure. Remind them of the need to lead up to a good ending.

Plenary

Invite pupils to share their plans and ask others to comment. Have they thought of a good ending? Support pupils who can't comment constructively by suggesting the 'I like ... I like ... I suggest ...' formula.

EXTENDED WRITING

Pupils use their plans to write the first draft of a story. Their response partners should comment on the story using the tips they wrote in Unit 2. Let children discuss as they write.

YOU WILL NEED

- Enlarged copy of one group's spider diagram from Lesson One
- Flipchart with headings: Introduction; Build-up; Climax; Resolution
- **PCM 7** – Story planner
- **Prompt Chart 1** – Response Partner Rules
- **Prompt Chart 2** – Planning a story

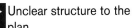

For activities linked to this lesson see **PAGE 102**

WATCH OUT FOR

- ▶ Unclear structure to the plan.
- ▶ Lack of relationship between the plan and their brainstorm notes.

Fantastic Mr Fox • PLAYSCRIPT

MAIN WRITING OBJECTIVE

- **To write playscripts based on known stories.** 4.1 T13

Word and sentence level objective

- To identify adverbs and understand their functions in sentences. 4.1 S4

LESSON ONE

MODEL TEXT

- Explain the lesson objective: *to look at the features of a playscript and prepare it for performance.*

- The play is based on *Fantastic Mr Fox* by Roald Dahl.

OHT 5

- Read aloud the first stage directions. Why are these stage directions so important? *they show where the scene is set and what the actors are doing*

- Allocate parts to confident readers and read through the play together. The whole class can join in with the chorus. Read the stage directions yourself.

- Ask pupils:
  – What are the characters doing? *Boggis, Bunce and Bean are sitting still in the background except when spoken about. The three children are sitting at the front of the stage talking about the farmers.*
  – Which words tell us about the farmers characters? *horrible, mean, nasty, dreaded*
  – How could these words be read?

Word and sentence level work

1 Ask pupils how they might chant the rhyme that opens the play. *merrily, cheekily, slowly.* Discuss how the different ways of chanting it could affect the whole tone of the opening.

2 The farmers eat revoltingly. What other adverbs could have been used here? *e.g. greedily, messily, horribly*

Group activities: differentiation

PCM 8

In groups of three, pupils prepare the scene for performance, using **PCM 8**. Give them ten minutes to discuss and mark the text, and ten minutes to practise it. Remind them NOT to read out the stage directions.

Guided reading. Help **lower attainers** to pick out clues as to how they should read.

Plenary

Invite a group to perform their play. Ask other pupils to comment on expression and the use of stage directions.

YOU WILL NEED

- **Pupil's Book** page 10
- **OHT 5** – Scene 1
- **PCM 8** – Scene 1
- **PCM 9** – Scene 1 continued.

 ICT For activities linked to this lesson see **PAGE 102**

HOMEWORK

Pupils read the next part of the scene on **PCM 9** then write down six words to describe each character. You will need to prepare by reading the text through with pupils before they go home.

Link to reading objectives

- To prepare, read and perform playscripts; to compare scripts with stories.   4.1 T5
- To chart the build-up of a play scene.   4.1 T6

Assumed prior knowledge

- To read, prepare and present playscripts.   3.1 T4
- To recognise the key differences between prose and plays.   3.1 T5

Pupil's Book page ● 10

Planning suggestion

This unit can be used as part of a week looking at plays. You might want to link it to a theatre visit. You could get the class to prepare a playscript and then perform it in front of another class, to parents or in assembly.

LESSON TWO

SHARED WRITING

- Invite pupils to share their homework words. Explain that it is helpful to know what characters are like when performing plays.

- Explain the lesson objective: *to write a playscript, using the next part of the story.*

- The three farmers are furious because Mr Fox has been stealing their chickens and ducks and turkeys. Read Chapter 2 aloud. Ask pupils:
  – Where does the scene start? *in the fox's hole* Which lines tell you?
  – Where do you think Boggis, Bunce and Bean are?

- Ask pupils to pick out the words that are spoken by Mr Fox. Underline them.

- With pupils, begin writing the play. Start with the setting.

- Which character speaks first? Write the opening dialogue, using the speech from the story. Ask pupils HOW Mr Fox might speak these words and add this in as a stage direction.

- Invite pupils to make up Mrs Fox's reply. Point out the conventions for setting out plays as you write.

- Write out some stage directions for what Mr Fox does. Help pupils to pick out clues from the text.

Group activities: differentiation

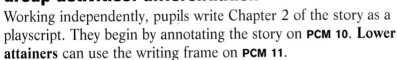

Working independently, pupils write Chapter 2 of the story as a playscript. They begin by annotating the story on **PCM 10**. **Lower attainers** can use the writing frame on **PCM 11**.

Guided writing. Help **higher attainers** to keep the story-line moving by using stage directions. Help **lower attainers** pick out dialogue and decide who is speaking.

Plenary

Invite groups to read aloud one pupil's playscript. Remind them to read with expression.

EXTENDED WRITING

Pupils finish writing their playscripts, then read them through in groups and add stage directions. They can then revise their scripts and practise for a final performance.

YOU WILL NEED

- **OHT 6** – Chapter 2/Play writing frame
- **PCM 10** – Story, Chapter 2
- **PCM 11** – Play writing frame

 For activities linked to this lesson see **PAGE 102**

WATCH OUT FOR

- ▶ Speech marks
- ▶ Use of *said*.
- ▶ Poor continuity of story-line.

5

Feathers Fly! • NEWSPAPER REPORT

MAIN WRITING OBJECTIVE

• **To write a newspaper style report, e.g. about school events or an incident from a story.**   4.1 T24

Word and sentence level objective

• To practise using commas to mark grammatical boundaries within sentences; link to work on editing and revising own writing.   4.1 S5

LESSON ONE

YOU WILL NEED

- **Pupil's Book** page 12
- **OHT 7** – A Hat Trick of Break-Ins
- **PCM 12** – Features of a newspaper report
- **PCM 13** – Homework

MODEL TEXT

• Explain the lesson objective: *to look at how newspaper reports present information.*

• Display the headline only. What part of a newspaper report is this? How do they know? *not a sentence, short and punchy*

• How is the report set out? *headline, writer's name, columns, paragraphs*

• Read the report aloud. Ask pupils:
  – Can you give a longer version of the headline? *Ashwood school has been broken into three times and lots of equipment stolen*
  – What does the first paragraph tell us? *it summarises the events*
  – What facts does the second paragraph give us? *the dates of the robberies and what was stolen*
  – Who did the writer interview? *the caretaker, the police*
  – What is the last paragraph about? *it says how people can help*

PB • Read aloud the report from the Pupil's Book in preparation for group work. Is it based on fact or fiction? *Fiction – Fantastic Mr Fox.* How did they guess?

Word and sentence level work

1 Ask a pupil to read aloud paragraph 2, pausing after each comma. Then ask another pupil to read it without the pauses. What is the difference?

2 Where else are commas used? *before and after speech in paragraph 5*

Group activities: differentiation

PCM 12 All pupils use **PCM 12** and do questions 1 and 2. **Higher attainers** move on to question 3 – writing the headline as a longer sentence.

Guided reading. Check that **lower attainers** understand the difference between fact and fiction.

Plenary

Which features would pupils find in a newspaper report? List some questions to ask Farmer Bean. Look at examples of the headline written as a longer sentence. Discuss the effect.

 ICT For activities linked to this lesson see **PAGE 103**

HOMEWORK

Pupils should fill in the missing punctuation in the report on **PCM 13**.

Link to reading objectives

● To identify the main features of newspapers.	4.1 T20
● To predict newspaper stories from the evidence of headlines.	4.1 T21

Assumed prior knowledge

● To explore ways of writing headlines.	3.2 T17
● To experiment with different ways of telling the same event e.g. a news report.	3.3 T22
● Familiarity with *Fantastic Mr Fox* by Roald Dahl (Unit 4).	

Planning suggestion

You could make 'the media' your theme for the week. Pupils can look at a variety of newspaper reports. They can then go on to put together their own class newspaper. You could link the reports to work in other subjects.

LESSON TWO

SHARED WRITING

- Briefly look at pupils' homework and remind them why commas and speech marks are so important.

- Explain the lesson objective: *to write a newspaper report.*

OHT 8

- Brainstorm a subject for your report. Choose either a real event, or an incident from a story they have read recently.

- Establish the main events: What happened? When? Where? Who was involved?

- Ask pupils who they might interview. Discuss the questions they would ask, and invent some answers.

- Brainstorm a punchy headline.

- With pupils, draft the first paragraph. Remind them that they need to summarise the events, and make people want to read on.

- Discuss and model how it can be improved – cross out, use arrows and insertion marks.

- Discuss what might go in other paragraphs.

Group activities: differentiation

PCM 14

All pupils should work independently on the first draft of their own report. **Lower attainers** can continue with the ideas from shared writing. A planning frame is provided on **PCM 14**.

Guided writing. Work with **higher attainers** on their first paragraphs. Does it summarise the events? Will it make readers want to know more?

Plenary

Invite pupils to read their headlines aloud. Comment on their style and the effect on the reader.

EXTENDED WRITING

Pupils finish drafting their reports, then swap with a partner and revise and edit. They then write a final version, laid out in columns and including a picture. **PCM 15** is provided for support.

YOU WILL NEED

- **OHT 8** – Report planning frame
- **PCM 14** – Report planning frame
- **PCM 15** – Report writing frame

For activities linked to this lesson see **PAGE 103**

WATCH OUT FOR
▶ Unfocused paragraphs.
▶ Speech marks in reported speech.
▶ Story writing.

6

The Evacuee • HISTORICAL NOVEL

MAIN WRITING OBJECTIVE

- **To write independently, linking own experience to situations in historical stories.**   4.1 T12

Word and sentence level objective

- To define familiar vocabulary in their own words, using alternative phrases or expressions.   4.1 W11

LESSON ONE

YOU WILL NEED

- **Pupil's Book** pages 14–15
- **PCM 16** – Character
- **PCM 17** – Homework

MODEL TEXT

- Explain the lesson objective: *to look at a chapter from a historical novel* – Tom's Private War, *by Robert Leeson.*

- The story is set in 1939, at the beginning of World War 2. Tom and his friends, Molly and William, live in the country. One day a group of evacuees arrive from Liverpool.

- Read the extract aloud. You could ask two confident pupils to take the parts of William and the evacuee. Can pupils guess what Tom's private war might be?
  Ask pupils:
  – How do you think the evacuees felt? *confused, sad, lonely, frightened*
  – What words tell us this? *pale, miserable, clutching cardboard suitcases*
  – Why did Widow Robertson take in the evacuee? *she lived on her own, no one else wanted him*
  – Why do you think no one wanted him? Look for clues in the text. *face like a ferret, sharp nose and red eyes, hard as nails*
  – Which words tell us what the evacuee thought about this new place? *dump, nothing here, useless*
  – How would you feel if you had to leave your home and go to stay in a strange place?

Word and sentence level work

1 Find examples of informal or slang words and phrases. *crying shame, snobs, jiggers, hard as nails, flicks, a bunch of ...*

2 Ask pupils to put these phrases into their own words. What would they say when they are with their friends?

Group activities: Differentiation

Lower attainers only complete question 1. All pupils complete questions 2–3. **Higher attainers** complete question 4, using **PCM 16**.

Guided reading. Do questions 2 and 3 orally with **lower attainers**.

Plenary

Invite **lower attainers** to read out and explain their answers. Ask **higher attainers** to suggest adjectives to describe William, Molly and the evacuee. Ask them to refer to the clues in the text.

ICT For activities linked to this lesson see **PAGE 103**

HOMEWORK

Ask pupils to imagine how they would have felt if they were the evacuee. They should fill in the chart on **PCM 17**.

Link to reading objectives

- To investigate how settings and characters are built up from small details, and how the reader responds to them. **4.1 T1**
- To identify the main characteristics of key characters. **4.1 T2**

Assumed prior knowledge

- To identify main characters; to evaluate their behaviour and justify opinions. **3.2 T3**
- To discuss characters' feelings and behaviour and make judgements about relationships. **3.3 T5**
- To write a character's account of incidents in a story. **3.3 T12**

Planning suggestion

The theme of the week could be the lives and relationships of children in different periods of history. Encourage pupils to think about historical situations, to empathise with characters, and to link their own experiences to those described.

LESSON TWO

SHARED WRITING

- Explain the lesson objective: *to write about how they would feel if they were an evacuee.*

- Ask pupils to imagine they have been sent away from home – maybe for several months. What would they miss? Brainstorm some ideas and jot them down under the headings on the flipchart.

- Ask pupils to think about how they would feel. They can use their homework notes to help them.

- Re-cap the main events from the extract: *arriving in a strange place; being 'chosen'; meeting the other children; not knowing about things and being laughed at*

- Choose one event. With pupils, brainstorm how they might have responded to it. Remind them to focus on their feelings as well as what they did.

- Draft a couple of sentences to describe that response. Model the use of descriptive details.

YOU WILL NEED

- Flipchart with headings:
  What I would miss.
  people   places   things
- **PCM 18** – Writing frame

Group activities: Differentiation

All pupils complete the task, imagining they are an evacuee during World War 2, and writing two paragraphs about their experience. **Lower attainers** can use the writing frame on **PCM 18** for support.

Guided writing. Work with **higher attainers**, helping them to empathise with the characters and situation, and to write detailed descriptions of their feelings.

Plenary

Ask several pupils to read aloud their work in progress. The rest of the class should comment, focusing particularly on the description of feelings and actions.

ICT For activities linked to this lesson see **PAGE 103**

EXTENDED WRITING

Ask pupils to plan a story in which they are an evacuee. They should include their description of how they felt, and try to write some dialogue. They write a first draft.

⚠ WATCH OUT FOR

- ▶ Inappropriate use of 3rd person.
- ▶ Lack of detail.
- ▶ Lack of empathy with character and situation.

7

Up and Away! • PARAGRAPHS

MAIN WRITING OBJECTIVE

- **To use paragraphs in story writing to organise and sequence the narrative.** 4.1 T15

Word and sentence level objectives

- To spell regular verb endings *-ed, -ing.* 4.1 W7
- To spell irregular tense changes, e.g. *go/went, can/could.* 4.1 W8

LESSON ONE

MODEL TEXT

- Explain the lesson objective: *to look at how paragraphs are used to build up a story.*

PB
- Read the extract aloud – invite pupils to read the dialogue. Explain that this is the opening chapter of a story.

- Look at the first few paragraphs in detail. Ask pupils:
  - Why is the first paragraph important? What does it tell us? *it sets the scene, tells you what went before, and hints at what might happen; mention of magic makes you want to read on*
  - What does paragraph 3 tell us? *where the kite came from, what it looked like, that it was really special*
  - What does paragraph 4 tell us? *what Philip's dad had said*
  - How do the next three paragraphs build up tension? *whispering voice in Philip's head encouraging him to sneak out, then he gives in*

- Ask pupils to sum up each of the paragraphs in one sentence, using the past tense.

Word and sentence level work

OHT 9
1 Ask pupils to find examples of verbs ending in *-ed.* e.g. *happened, listened, laughed, wanted.* What tense are they? Change them into present tense.
2 Changing tenses in some words is not quite so simple. Ask pupils to identify some irregular verbs, e.g. *saw, blown, brought.* Change these into the present tense.
3 Look for different examples of other verb endings e.g. *whisper<u>ing</u>*

Group activities: differentiation

Pupils work in mixed ability groups, each with a good reader, and focus on the second part of the extract. They use **PCM 19** to write captions summarising each paragraph.

Plenary

Ask a pupil from each group to read aloud their paragraph captions. Others comment on whether the main points of each paragraph have been covered. Briefly discuss how these paragraphs move the story on.

YOU WILL NEED
- **Pupil's Book** pages 17–18
- **OHT 9** – First part of extract.
- **PCM 19** – Paragraph captions
- **PCM 20** – Homework

ICT For activities linked to this lesson see **PAGE 103**

HOMEWORK

All pupils fill in the missing verbs on **PCM 20. Higher attainers** can go on to the last task, writing verbs into sentences.

Link to reading objective	
● To explore narrative order, mapping out the main stages: introduction, build-up, climax or conflict and resolution.	4.1 T4

Assumed prior knowledge	
● To identify and evaluate behaviour of characters.	3.2 T3
● To identify significant aspects of a text, e.g. opening, build-up.	3.3 T2

Planning suggestion

You may wish to explore the use of paragraphs to organise stories, before moving on to look at their use in other subject areas/text types. Concentrate on how they are used to organise and order the text.

LESSON TWO

SHARED WRITING

- Go over the homework and recap verb tenses.

- Explain the lesson objective: *to plan the next part of Philip's adventure using paragraphs.*

- Suggest that their story should follow on from the last paragraph in their books.

- Give pupils two minutes to talk about what might happen next. *he could meet a big bird, a helicopter, or land on a tall building*

- Jot down pupils ideas on a flipchart, then choose one to use for shared writing.

- Discuss how you might organise the information using paragraphs. You could use a paragraph to focus on thoughts and feelings. Make brief notes for each paragraph on the chart.

- Remind pupils about building up to a problem or climax – the most exciting part of the story.

- Ask pupils to suggest how the story might end – the resolution. How does Philip get home?

- Explain that this is the 'bones' or 'skeleton' of the story. Each step will be a paragraph and, when they write, they can add in lots of details to make it more exciting.

Group activities: differentiation

All pupils continue planning paragraphs to complete the story. They can use **PCM 21** to help them. **Lower attainers** can finish the outline begun in shared writing and begin to write the first two paragraphs.

Guided writing. Help **higher attainers** to use paragraphs to build climax and resolution.

Plenary

Ask some **higher attainers** to read their plans aloud. Comment briefly on their ideas. Ask **lower attainers** to read their paragraphs.

EXTENDED WRITING

Pupils finish drafting their stories, based on their plan using paragraphs to organise. They then swap drafts with a partner, and suggest how each others' work can be improved.

YOU WILL NEED

- **OHT 10** – Story steps
- Flipchart
- **PCM 21** – Story steps
- **Prompt Chart 2** – Planning a story
- **Prompt Chart 3** – Descriptive writing

For activities linked to this lesson see **PAGE 103**

WATCH OUT FOR
▶ Unclear focus in paragraphs.
▶ Limited use of plan when drafting.

MAIN WRITING OBJECTIVE

- **To write poems based on personal experience, linked to poems read; to experiment with powerful and expressive verbs.** 4.1 T14

Word and sentence level objectives

- To identify powerful verbs. 4.1 S3
- To revise verb tenses. 4.1 S2
- To revise synonyms from Year 3.

LESSON ONE

MODEL TEXT

- Explain the lesson objective: *to read and discuss poems about cats.*

- Ask pupils to close their eyes and imagine a cat. What does it look and feel like? How does it move?

- The three poems all concentrate on a cat's movements. Read the poems aloud.

- Ask pupils to pick out the verbs in 'Catalog'.

- Mime the movements being described, encouraging pupils to join in.

- Look at 'Cat Kenning'. A 'kenning' is an Anglo-Saxon poem which describes something without saying what it is. Ask pupils:
  – How is the poem laid out? *Each line is made out of two words put together. The second word is made out of a verb.*

- Read 'I see a cat'. What does this poem describe? *the moment just before a cat pounces* How is it different from the other poems? *it's like a frozen moment, or photograph*

Word and sentence level work

1 Look at the powerful verbs in 'I see a cat'. *poised, pounce, crouched, strikes* What happens if you use other verbs, e.g. *waiting* instead of *poised*? Can pupils see why the verbs are so powerful?

2 Explore the similes: 'eyes . . . hard as jewels', 'like a coiled spring' and 'tail like a finger beckoning'. Ask pupils to explain them in their own words.

Group activities: differentiation

Working in pairs, all pupils complete both questions.

Guided reading. Encourage pupils to be as specific as they can about why they like a particular poem best.

Plenary

Take a class vote on the favourite poem and discuss reasons.

YOU WILL NEED

- **Pupil's Book** page 20
- **PCM 22** – Homework

ICT For activities linked to this lesson see **PAGE 103**

HOMEWORK

Ask pupils to make notes about an animal they know well using **PCM 22**. Explain that they will be writing a poem about it in the next session so they will need to think of some powerful words to describe it.

Link to reading objective

- To compare and contrast poems on similar themes, particularly their forms and language, discussing personal responses and preferences. 4.1 T7

Assumed prior knowledge

- Calligrams and shape poems. 3.1
- Riddles. 3.3
- Verb tenses. 3.1 S4

Pupil's Book page ● 20

Planning suggestion

Link the poetry writing to topic work on animals in other subjects such as science or art. This background work will help those pupils who need information about an animal before they can write a poem.

LESSON TWO

SHARED WRITING

- Explain the lesson objective: *to write an animal poem modelled on one of the 'cat' poems read.*

- Briefly discuss some of the notes made for homework. Choose a familiar animal as the subject for a class poem. Ask pupils to close their eyes and imagine the way it looks and feels, and how it moves.

- Brainstorm some words and phrases to describe the animal. What is it doing? What does it look like? How does it move? Concentrate on powerful verbs, and words which really help to create a picture.

- Ask pupils to think of similes. What could you compare the animal's fur or skin to? Is there something that moves in a similar way?

- Start to structure the ideas into a poem, using the writing frame. Start the lines with different parts of speech.

- Change the writing frame to suit your needs, and encourage pupils to do the same. Add powerful verbs. You could add or delete questions, or swap the order of them round.

- Discuss the problem of writing the last lines. Try to think of a sudden movement or event, or add a line that sums up the animal perfectly. Or repeat the first line.

Group activities: differentiation

All pupils draft their own animal poem using 'I see a cat' as a model, then exchange their work with a response partner. (A writing frame is provided on **PCM 23** if needed.)
If they wish, pupils can write a kenning.

Guided writing. Work with pupils on the use of powerful verbs. Alternatively you could scribe a group poem with **lower attainers**.

Plenary

Listen to some first drafts, and invite comments and suggestions for improvement. Discuss the response partner work.

EXTENDED WRITING

Pupils revise and refine their poems, then make a class display with animal pictures and photographs.

YOU WILL NEED

- Flipchart
- **OHT 11** – Writing frame
- **PCM 23** – Writing frame
- **Prompt Chart 4** – Writing poetry

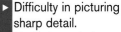

For activities linked to this lesson see
PAGE 103

WATCH OUT FOR

- ▶ Difficulty in picturing sharp detail.
- ▶ Limited vocabulary.

Young Archaeologist

● MAGAZINE REPORT

MAIN WRITING OBJECTIVE

- **To write a non-chronological report, including the use of organisational devices, e.g. numbered lists and headings.** 4.1 T27

Word and sentence level objective

- To revise work on verb tenses. 4.1 S2

LESSON ONE

MODEL TEXT

- Explain the lesson objective: *to look at a magazine, investigating features and layout.*

- Explain that the extracts are taken from the magazine of the *Young Archaeologist Club*. Do pupils know what an archaeologist is?

- Ask pupils to scan the spread. What kinds of writing are there? *report, competition, jokes*
  – What is the purpose of each? *to inform (report) and entertain (competition and jokes)*

- Read the report aloud. Ask pupils:
  – Who wrote this report?
  – What facts does she give in her report? *age of things, what they looked like, reasons for the buildings being there*
  – Who might find this report interesting? *children who like history or archaeology or travel*
  – How does Claire end her report? *with an opinion, recommending the place to other archaeology fans*

Word and sentence level work

1 Highlight the verbs in paragraphs 2 and 3 (mostly *is* and *are*). What tense are most of them in? *present*

2 Change these verbs to the past tense. e.g. *There was a rock on the island* … What effect does this have? *makes it sound like the rock no longer exists*

Group activities: differentiation

All pupils do questions 1 and 2. **Higher attainers** can go on to question 3.

Plenary

Talk about the audience for the magazine. How does this affect the way it is written?

YOU WILL NEED

- **Pupil's Book** pages 22–23
- **OHT 12** – Claire's report

ICT For activities linked to this lesson see **PAGE 104**

HOMEWORK

Ask pupils to look through magazines or newspapers for examples of reports. Ask them to look for examples of interesting layouts, use of headings etc.

Link to reading objectives

- To identify features of non-fiction texts in print, e.g headings, lists, captions, bullet points.   4.1 T17
- To identify the features of magazine articles including lay-out, information, voice, formality, organisation.   4.1 T20

Assumed prior knowledge

- To be able to write simple non-chronological reports.   3.1 T23
- To write non-fiction texts using headings, captions etc.   2.3 T20

Planning suggestion

The focus for the week could be different media: magazine articles, news reports and advertisements. Compare the different types of article, looking at purpose, layout, formality and intended audience.

LESSON TWO

SHARED WRITING

- Spend a short time looking at the pieces collected by pupils. Comment on the layout, purpose and audience.

- Explain the lesson objective: *to write a report for a class magazine, linked to topic work or work in another subject.*

- Discuss what you are going to write about.

- Talk about who will read the magazine – Parents? Younger children? It is important to keep the audience in mind as you write.

- Brainstorm ideas for what you might include in the report. Jot all the ideas down, then highlight the main subject areas, e.g. *Ancient Greece: buildings, clothes, customs*

- Using these main points as paragraph headings, demonstrate how to group similar facts in paragraphs.

- With pupils, write the opening paragraph. Model the use of the present tense.

- Ask pupils how they could present the information to make it easier to follow. Look at some of the devices in the articles they have found – headings, lists with bullet points etc.

Group activities: differentiation

Working in pairs, all pupils draft a report for a magazine based on the class brainstorm. **Higher attainers** can do some extra research if necessary. **Lower attainers** can use the planning frame on **PCM 23** to help them.

Guided writing. Make sure pupils are clear about the purpose and audience of their writing.

Plenary

Invite pupils to share their work so far. Evaluate against the features on the **Prompt Chart**.

EXTENDED WRITING

Pupils finish drafting their reports, then swap with a partner and make any changes. Encourage them to give the final version an eye-catching heading and to think about layout. They could add jokes or a competition.

YOU WILL NEED

- Books and information on subject chosen for report
- **Prompt Chart 5** – Information texts
- **OHT 13** – Report planning frame
- Flipchart
- **PCM 24** – Report planning frame

ICT For activities linked to this lesson see **PAGE 104**

WATCH OUT FOR

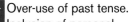

- ▶ Over-use of past tense.
- ▶ Inclusion of personal pronouns.
- ▶ Little awareness of audience.

MAIN WRITING OBJECTIVE

- **To write poems based on personal experience, linked to poems read.**   4.1 T14

Word and sentence level objectives

- To revise work on verb tenses.   4.1 S2
- To identify adverbs.   4.1 S4

LESSON ONE

MODEL TEXT

YOU WILL NEED

- **Pupil's Book** page 24
- **OHT 14** – Poems
- **PCM 25** – Comparing poems
- **PCM 26** – Homework

- Explain the lesson objective: *to look at how poetry says a lot in a few words, and is a good way of expressing moods and feelings.*

- Explain that Yolande and Jeffrey read a poem which began, 'I have a wolf in me . . .' in which the poet described a wild feeling inside him. They then used his poem as a model to write their own.

- Read their poems aloud. Ask pupils:
  - What feelings was Yolande describing in her poem? *feeling shy, hiding away from things, being quiet and peaceful*
  - How does a deer fit Yolande? *deers are shy, quiet animals and move around almost unseen*
  - What is the mood of her poem? What words tell you?
  - How does Jeffrey describe himself? *active, rushing around, annoying people*
  - Why did he choose a beetle? *beetles scuttle around, irritate people*
  - Which poem do they like best? Why? Have they ever felt like that?

Word and sentence level work

1 Look at Yolande's poem in more detail. Highlight all the verbs.

2 Ask pupils to identify the words which describe HOW the deer is doing things, e.g. *shyly, peacefully, quietly.* Introduce the term **adverb** – adverbs 'add to the verb' by describing how something is done. They usually end in *-ly.*

3 Yolande put some adverbs in front and some after the verb. Why did she put 'peacefully' and 'quietly' in front of the verb? *sound more important? The rhythm is better?* What happens if you change their position?

Group activities: differentiation

Working in pairs, pupils decide which poem they like best. They then fill in the comments on **PCM 25** giving reasons for their choice.

Guided reading. Work with **lower attainers** to answer the questions orally.

Plenary

Take a class vote on the favourite poem and explore the reasons why pupils liked it best.

ICT | For activities linked to this lesson see **PAGE 104**

HOMEWORK

Pupils use **PCM 26** to add adverbs to verbs. **Lower attainers** can do question 1 only.

Link to reading objective

- To compare and contrast poems on a similar theme, discussing personal responses and preferences.   4.1 T7

Assumed prior knowledge

- General experience of poetry.
- To read poetry, comparing different views of the same subject.   3.1 T6
- Talking and writing about mood and feeling.

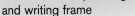

Planning suggestion

This unit can be used as part of a week exploring poetry. It links to Unit 8. You could produce a class anthology of poems on a similar theme, including both poems read and pupils' own work.

LESSON TWO

SHARED WRITING

- Explain the lesson objective: *to write their own 'mood and feeling' poems, using the poems read as models.*

- Remind pupils of the poems they read previously.

- Brainstorm some moods or feelings, e.g. *bored, angry, excited, silly.* What animals could you associate with these moods? What are they doing? e.g. *bored: cow chewing grass; angry: wasp buzzing around some food; excited: puppy chasing his tail*

- Choose one mood and an animal to illustrate it. Ask pupils to suggest some verbs and adverbs which illustrate the mood.

- Using the writing frame, start to shape the first few lines of the poem, using the model 'I have a .... in me'. Show pupils how to alter the frame if they need to.

- As you write, model deleting words that don't work, and experimenting with different adverbs to get the right mood.

- Discuss the last line. It needs to round off the poem. It could sum up your mood, or show how people react when you're in that mood.

Group activities: differentiation

In pairs, pupils brainstorm ideas for their own mood poem. They then work on their own to write their poems. All pupils can use one of the writing frames on **PCM 27** for support if they need it.

Guided writing. Work with **lower attainers** helping them to think of powerful verbs and adverbs to capture their mood.

Plenary

Ask pupils to read their work in progress. Others comment. Model a good response partner routine: positive comments followed by suggestions for improvement.

EXTENDED WRITING

Pupils finish drafting their mood poems then swap with a partner and revise. They make final copies of their poems which could be used as part of a presentation or assembly on feelings.

YOU WILL NEED

- **OHT 15** – Poem planning and writing frame
- **PCM 27** – Poem writing frames
- **Prompt Chart 4** – Writing poetry

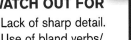 For activities linked to this lesson see **PAGE 104**

WATCH OUT FOR
▶ Lack of sharp detail.
▶ Use of bland verbs/ adverbs.

MAIN WRITING OBJECTIVES

- **To write clear instructions by using linking phrases and organisational devices.**   4.1 T25
- **To improve the cohesion of written instructions and directions**   4.1 T26

Word and sentence level objectives

- To revise verb tenses.   4.1 S2
- To identify adverbs.   4.1 S4

LESSON ONE

MODEL TEXT

- Explain the lesson objective: *to look at a map and directions for a bike ride, and discuss the features of written directions.*

- Giving directions is a form of instruction. Why it is so important to be clear when giving directions? *so people don't get lost*

- Ask pupils to give a simple set of directions, e.g. to the school library.

- Look at the map. Give pupils a few minutes to interpret it. How easy is the map to follow?

- Read the written directions aloud. Ask a pupil to point to features on the map as they are mentioned.
  - Was the map easier to follow with the written directions?
  - Could you have followed the directions without the map?
  - What are the symbols for bridge, gate, house and church. Would it help to have them in the key?
  - What else could be included on the map to help people find their way? *e.g. numbered points along the route, an idea of distance*

- Look at the written directions. Ask pupils to pick out the features of instructional writing. *you will need, verbs to start sentences (imperative tense), linking phrases/connectives such as 'after'*

Word and sentence level work

1 Ask pupils to pick out the verbs used in the written directions. Discuss their position in the sentence and the use of the present tense.

2 Ask pupils to find two adverbs in the text. *slowly, carefully* How do these help the bike rider? *tell you HOW to ride on the terrain*

Group activities: differentiation

Pupils work in pairs to write directions for the rest of the bike ride.
Lower attainers can use **PCM 28** for support.

Guided reading. Check pupils' understanding of the map symbols.

Plenary

Ask a pair of pupils to read out their directions while another pair follow the route on the OHT.

YOU WILL NEED

- **Pupil's Book** pages 26–27
- **OHT 16** – Map
- **PCM 28** – Map
- **PCM 29** – Homework

ICT For activities linked to this lesson see **PAGE 104**

HOMEWORK

Pupils suggest what the map symbols on **PCM 28** mean. If appropriate, encourage them to look at any maps they might have at home.
Answers (left to right): house, wood, road, church, path, railway line, bridge, lane, river.

Link to reading objective

- To identify the features of instructional texts.   4.1 T22

Assumed prior knowledge

- Instructions.   3.2 T16
- Notemaking.   3.2 T17
- Verb tenses.   3.1 S4

Planning suggestion

This unit can be used as part of a week's work on writing instructions. The work can be linked to topic work in another subject such as ICT or geography.

LESSON TWO

SHARED WRITING

- Explain the lesson objective: *to write directions for a local walk.*

- Try and provide a real purpose for the writing. It could be part of a local guide.

- Ask pupils for ideas of places they could walk in or around the local area. Keep it simple and short. It could be to the shops, along a river, or from school to a local place of interest.

- You could ask them to work from memory, but if possible, display an enlarged copy of a local map. Mark the route with a coloured pen, including a clear start and finish.

- Ask pupils to identify some of the main landmarks or things to look out for along the route. Explain that these can be used to identify the different stages of the walk. Number them (maximum of 5).

- Work out the rough distances – this is very important! Refer to the scale on the map if it has one.

- Add a simple key, drawing symbols on the map.

- Draft a 'You will need' box, e.g. *wellingtons, bus fare home, money for the sweet shop on the way!*

- With pupils, draft the first stage. Model opening the sentence with a verb, and number the written instructions to correspond with the numbered stage on the map.

Group activities: differentiation

In pairs, pupils draft directions for the walk discussed in shared writing. **Higher attainers** could choose an alternative route. Write any key words or spellings on the board.

Guided writing. Work on clarity and conciseness and encourage pupils to test out what they've written as they go along.

Plenary

Ask pairs to read out their directions while others follow on the map. How easy are they to follow?

EXTENDED WRITING

Pupils finish drafting their directions, then draw their own map, adding a key, arrows etc. Try out the directions on pupils from another class.

YOU WILL NEED

- Enlarged photocopy or OHT of map of local area (optional)

 For activities linked to this lesson see **PAGE 104**

WATCH OUT FOR

- ▶ Confused or overlong sentences.
- ▶ Lack of logical sequence.
- ▶ Inaccurate numbering.

MAIN WRITING OBJECTIVE

- **To write descriptive, expressive language based on reading, linked to work on adjectives and similes.**   4.2 T13

Word and sentence level objectives

- To revise and extend work on adjectives.   4.2 S1
- To use commas, connectives and full stops to join and separate clauses.   4.2 S4

LESSON ONE

MODEL TEXT

- Explain the lesson objective: *to look at the detailed description in an extract from* The Iron Woman *and explore how it builds tension.*

PB • Ted Hughes is a poet as well as a writer of stories. Read the extract aloud. (A 'drain' is a small canal dug to help drain the marshes.)

- Ask pupils to describe the mood of the extract. *tense, scary*

OHT 17 • How does the language create mood? Focus on the first half of the extract. Ask pupils to pick out the scary details *lonely place, black water, bottomless black*

- Find words which tell us what Lucy is feeling. *loneliness; fear*

- Discuss rhythm and ask them to pick out powerful details. *'twirling little whorls of light'; 'bottomless black'; 'toes curling like claws and the soles of her feet pricking with electricity'*

PB • How is the mystery built up? *things moving/being disturbed but we don't know why, the wailing cry*

- Who is asking the questions in lines 29–33? How does this add to the tension? *because we feel panicky like Lucy*

- Can the pupils guess what is coming out of the water?

Word and sentence level work

OHT 17 1 Ask pupils to point out the adjectives used in the first paragraph. *lonely place; bluish, pinky sky; soft cloud; black water*

2 Look at the contrast between short and long sentences. Highlight *'Then it came again'*. Why is it so short? Find another example.

3 Ask pupils to highlight the connectives and discuss how they move the story along: *now, as, then*. Explore the many different ways sentences are joined together.

Group activities: differentiation

PCM 30 Close reading activities. **Lower attainers** work on **PCM 30**; **higher attainers** work on **PCM 31**.

PCM 31

Plenary

Ask pairs of pupils to share their favourite words and phrases, and to say why they are effective descriptions. Introduce the homework.

YOU WILL NEED

- **Pupil's Book** pages 29–30
- **OHT 17** – First half of extract
- **PCM 30** – Close reading (lower attainers)
- **PCM 31** – Close reading (higher attainers)
- **PCM 32** – Next part of the story

 ICT For activities linked to this lesson see **PAGE 104**

HOMEWORK

Pupils need to read the next part of the story on **PCM 32** in preparation for writing. **Lower attainers** may need help from someone at home. If the text can't be read as homework, you will need to find time to read it aloud before the next lesson.

Link to reading objective

- To understand how the use of expressive and descriptive language can create moods, build tension and describe emotions.   4.2 T4

Assumed prior knowledge

- To write stories, building tension, creating mood and setting scenes.   3.3 T11
- Story settings.   3.1 T1

Planning suggestion

This unit can be used during a week focusing on *The Iron Woman* and its prequel *The Iron Man*.

LESSON TWO

SHARED WRITING

- Recap the homework text. Remind pupils of things that help make good writing – detail, using your senses etc. Give examples from the text.

- Explain the lesson objective: *to write a tense and scary description of your own meeting with the Iron Woman. Pupils should write in the first person.*

- Use the planning frame to make brief notes with pupils.

- Ask pupils for words and phrases to capture the atmosphere of the marshes. Encourage them to think about how they might feel as well as what they might see and hear. Brainstorm the first sentences.

- Collect words and phrases to describe the Iron Woman as she rises slowly out of the water. Ask pupils to think about how they would react, and to describe physical symptoms.

- Write a couple of opening sentences together. Model the use of really descriptive language.

- Encourage pupils to search the model for effects to imitate in their own writing: short sentences, new paragraphs, questions, vivid detail, similes. You can display the **Prompt Chart** to help them.

Group activities: differentiation

All pupils write part of a story: Meeting the Iron Woman. **Lower attainers** may use the writing frame on **PCM 33**. Pupils discuss their drafts with a response partner.

Guided writing. Help pupils to really 'see' what they describe by questioning them for precise detail.

Plenary

Ask pupils to read their drafts as dramatically as possible. Comment on effective words and phrases. Suggest improvements.

EXTENDED WRITING

Pupils continue to revise and refine their descriptions. If possible, pupils read further extracts from the novel before writing another section.

YOU WILL NEED

- **OHT 18** – Story planning frame
- **PCM 33** – Writing frame
- **Prompt Chart 3** – Descriptive writing

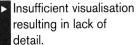

ICT For activities linked to this lesson see **PAGE 104**

WATCH OUT FOR

- ▶ Insufficient visualisation resulting in lack of detail.
- ▶ Limited use of adjectives and adverbs.

13 How does it work? ● EXPLANATION

MAIN WRITING OBJECTIVES

- To improve the cohesion of written explanations through paragraphing and the use of linking phrases and organisational devices such as headings and numbering.   4.2 T24
- To write explanations of a process, using conventions identified through reading.   4.2 T25

Word and sentence level objectives

- To recognise how commas, connectives and full stops are used to join and separate clauses.   4.2 S4

LESSON ONE

MODEL TEXT

- Explain the lesson objective: *to identify the key features of a written explanation.*

- Remind pupils that an explanation tells you *how* and *why* something happens and has to be really clear. Ask pupils where they have seen texts that explain things. *science, geography or other information books*

- Look at the extract together. Read the extract aloud, referring to the boxes and diagram details as you do so. Ask pupils:
  - Where does it tell you what the explanation is about? *introductory sentence at the top*
  - How do you know where to start reading? *the boxes are numbered*
  - How does the drawing help you to understand? *It shows you what the different parts of the vacuum cleaner look like and where they are.*

- Ask individual pupils to sum up what each box explains.

- Why do you think 'BURSTS' is in capital letters? *emphasises how important it is to empty the bag*

- Using the **Prompt Chart** summarise the key features of an explanation. Which of these features are included in the extract? *pictures, labels, short paragraphs, numbered points*

Word and sentence level work

1 Pick out words and phrases that are useful in writing explanations. *So; Once the; As the; Because; And as; But*

2 Look at the use of short sentences and commas to make meaning clear. How does the example 'just like a straw' help?

Group activities: differentiation

In paris, all pupils draw and label their own diagram of a vacuum cleaner. They then use it to explain to a partner, in their own words, how a vacuum cleaner works, pointing to the different parts of the diagram.
Lower attainers could label the diagram on **PCM 34**.

Guided reading. Focus on explaining how things happen and why, and in getting pupils to think about the logical order of an explanation.

Plenary

Listen to some pupils give their explanations. How clear are they?

YOU WILL NEED

- **Pupil's Book** pages 32–33
- **Prompt Chart 6** – Explanation
- **PCM 34** – How a vacuum cleaner works

ICT For activities linked to this lesson see **PAGE 105**

HOMEWORK

Ask pupils to make a drawing of a simple machine – it could be a kettle, a can opener, a stapler, or something as simple as a pencil sharpener. Ask them to think about how it works, and to make brief notes – they could ask an adult. Don't worry about the technical aspects.

Link to reading objective

- To identify the key features of explanatory texts – purpose, structure, language features, presentation.   4.2 T20

Assumed prior knowledge

- To compare the way information is presented.   3.1 T20
- Instructions.   4.1 T25/26
- The features of non-fiction texts.   4.1 T17

Planning suggestion

You can use this unit as part of a week looking at written explanations. The task can be linked to work in science, geography or design technology.

LESSON TWO

SHARED WRITING

- Look at some of the pupils' labelled drawings. Choose the clearest to be the focus of the shared writing. Choose something simple and familiar so that pupils can concentrate on the literary features of an explanation. Don't try to explain the technical aspects!

- Explain the lesson objective: *to write an explanation of how a simple machine works in the style of 'Until I met Dudley'.*

- Brainstorm all the features of an explanation. Use the **Prompt Chart** for support.

- Using the writing frame, begin to draft an explanation. Ask pupils for suggestions about what happens and why, but model the writing yourself. Discuss any difficulties you have (it's quite difficult to write a good, clear explanation!). If necessary, change the frame to make it fit what you want to say.

- Model reading through and revising the writing as you work, e.g. shortening sentences, adding commas for clarity, using connecting words and phrases, numbering points, etc.

Group activities: differentiation

Pupils work in pairs to plan and write their own explanation based on their homework notes. They can use the writing frame provided on **PCM 35**. **Lower attainers** can continue the explanation from shared writing.

Guided writing. Help pupils to keep sentences short. Concentrate on connectives, logical sequence and paragraphing.

Plenary

Listen to some of the work in progress. Comment on the clarity of the explanation and the use of key features from the **Prompt Chart**.

EXTENDED WRITING

Pupils swap drafts with a partner and discuss how their explanation can be improved. They then write a final version, with a clearly labelled drawing/diagram.

YOU WILL NEED

- **OHT 19** – Explanation writing frame
- **PCM 35** – Explanation writing frame
- **Prompt Chart 6** – Explanation

 For activities linked to this lesson see **PAGE 105**

WATCH OUT FOR
▶ Muddled sequence.
▶ Imprecise language.

- **To develop use of settings, making use of work on adjectives and figurative language to describe them.** 4.2 T10

- **To extend work on adjectives and adjectival phrases.** 4.2 S1

LESSON ONE

MODEL TEXT

YOU WILL NEED
- **Pupil's Book** pages 35–36
- **OHT 20** – Setting
- **PCM 36** – Homework

- Explain the lesson objective: *to look at a description of an imaginary setting.*

- Pupils may have seen the famous film 'The Wizard of Oz'. What do they remember about it? Summarise the story if needed: when a cyclone hits her Kansas home, Dorothy is whirled away to the magic land of Oz. She follows the yellow brick road, and meets the Scarecrow, the Tin Woodman and the Cowardly Lion. Finally, she arrives at the wonderful Emerald City of Oz. The Guardian of the Gates gives them special spectacles so they won't be dazzled by the sight of the City . . .

- Read the extract aloud. Ask pupils:
  – What is unusual about the Emerald City? *everything is green, even the people*
  – Does it sound like a friendly or unfriendly place? Ask pupils to find clues in the text. *'everyone seemed happy and contented and prosperous', the girl bows to Dorothy*

- Ask pupils to describe the shop windows, then to imagine going inside the sweet shop and the clothes shop. What other shops might there be in the Emerald City?

- Dorothy gets into the magic world of Oz by a cyclone. Discuss devices used in other stories to get into imaginary worlds, e.g. *rabbit hole, wardrobe*

Word and sentence level work

1 Ask pupils to find adjectives and adjectival phrases which help the reader 'see' the dazzling setting. *dazzled, brilliancy, glittering in the brightness of the sun*

2 Ask pupils to define 'brilliancy', 'studded' and 'prosperous'.

Group activities: differentiation

Working in pairs all pupils write or draw a description of Dorothy's room. **Higher attainers** can go on to draw a map of the setting.

ICT For activities linked to this lesson see **PAGE 105**

Plenary

Ask one or two pupils to read their descriptions. Then read the actual description from the Pupil's Book (lines 34–47). Compare the two and invite comments.

HOMEWORK

Pupils complete the activity on **PCM 36**.

Link to reading objectives	
● To understand how writers create imaginary worlds.	4.2 T1
● To compare and contrast settings.	4.2 T3

Assumed prior knowledge	
● Story settings.	3.1 T1
● Story maps.	3.2 T7

Planning suggestion

You could spend a week looking at a range of story settings so that pupils develop a repertoire. Explore how certain characters are linked to certain settings e.g. witch, alien.

LESSON TWO

SHARED WRITING

● Remind pupils about the Emerald City of Oz and the details which made it seem fantastical.

● Explain the lesson objective: *to write a description of a setting for a fantasy story.*

● Make improvements to the extract, taking suggestions from pupils' homework ideas. As you work, ask whether the additions or changes help the reader to see and feel the atmosphere of the place. Use prompt questions such as: What kind of door was it? Were there noises or shadows? What words would be better than 'loads of weeds'? e.g. *clambering ivy, overhanging vines*

● Encourage pupils to use all their senses to really bring the setting alive.

● Explain that you don't need to say 'It was spooky' – your description should show that.

● What details could you add to show that this is no ordinary castle?

● When you have added in all the ideas, read the passage again. It may now be over-written. If necessary, show pupils how to edit out some of the adjectives, choosing the ones that are really powerful.

Group activities: differentiation

Pupils draft a description of a magician's room and then discuss it with a partner. They can use **PCM 37** to support their planning. **Lower attainers** could continue working on the extract from Shared Writing. **Guided writing:** Work with pupils on the details, helping them to choose unusual adjectives and adjectival phrases to really bring the setting alive.

Plenary

Read through some of the descriptions. Can pupils picture the setting in their heads? Can they suggest improvements?

EXTENDED WRITING

Pupils can develop the setting into a story by brainstorming character ideas and possible plot outlines.

YOU WILL NEED
● **OHT 21** – Setting
● **PCM 37** – Planning frame
● **Prompt Chart 3** – Descriptive writing

ICT For activities linked to this lesson see **PAGE 105**

WATCH OUT FOR
▶ Lack of sharply-realised detail.

MAIN WRITING OBJECTIVE

- **To write poetry based on the structure and style of poems read, taking account of patterns of rhyme.** 4.2 T11

Word and sentence level objectives

- To read and spell words through identifying phonemes and syllabic patterns. 4.2 W1
- To understand how words have changed over time. 4.2 W11
- To revise and extend work on adjectives, linking to expressive language. 4.2 S1

LESSON ONE

YOU WILL NEED

- **Pupil's Book** page 38
- **OHT 22** – Henry King
- **PCM 38** – Henry King
- **PCM 39** – Comparison chart

MODEL TEXT

- Explain the lesson objective: *to look at poems with rhyming patterns.*

- Introduce the term 'Cautionary Tale'. Ask pupils to guess its meaning. Cautionary tales were very popular in Victorian times. They warned children of the horrible fates that would befall them if they were naughty.

- Read 'Henry King' aloud. Ask pupils:
  - How did Henry die? *from eating string which tangled up inside him*
  - Could it really happen?
  - What are children being cautioned about in this poem? *eating things they shouldn't*

- What do pupils notice about the rhyme pattern? Introduce and explain the term 'rhyming couplet'. Ask pupils to mark the rhyme scheme on the OHT (AA BB CC etc). Clap the rhythm together.

- Read the poem again together. Encourage pupils to be really melodramatic! Try different voices for Henry and the physicians.

- Read 'The Story of Augustus' in preparation for group activities.

Word and sentence level work

1 Ask pupils to mark examples of rhymes where the phoneme is the same but the spelling is different: *tied/inside; fees/disease; dead/bed*

2 Identify words and phrases not often used today – *physician, lamenting, untimely death, human frame, expires*. Substitute modern words, and discuss how this affects the tone of the poem.

Group activities: differentiation

Leave 'Henry King' on display, or hand out **PCM 38**. Working in pairs, pupils compare the two poems using **PCM 39**. They then practise performing 'The Story of Augustus'.

Higher attainers can go on to question 2, listing the rhyming couplets.

ICT For activities linked to this lesson see **PAGE 105**

Plenary

Ask pupils to feedback the rhyming couplets from 'The Story of Augustus'. This poem also has a chorus. Ask pupils to read it out in a suitably hysterical voice! Compare rhythm with 'Henry King'. Briefly recap the key features of cautionary tales.

HOMEWORK

Give pupils a copy of 'Henry King' (**PCM 38**) and ask them to learn it by heart.

Link to reading objective

- To identify rhyming couplets and read aloud effectively.   4.2 T7

Assumed prior knowledge

- Experience of a range of humorous and rhyming poetry.
- Adjectives.   3.2 S2

Planning suggestion

This unit can be used as part of a week looking at different rhyming patterns in poetry, e.g. couplets, limericks, choruses etc.

LESSON TWO

SHARED WRITING

- Listen to children recite the poem learnt for homework.

- Explain the lesson objective: *to write their own 'cautionary tale' poem.*

 OHT 22

- Recap all the key features of a cautionary tale, and remind pupils about rhyming couplets.

OHT 23

- Display the planning frame, and show pupils how to use it.

- Brainstorm some ideas for bad habits. e.g *always late, greedy, chews her pen*

- When you've decided on the crime, think of a name for the naughty child. Remind pupils that the surname must rhyme with the crime! e.g. *Gloria Benn/chews her pen*

- What happens in the tale? Discuss possible gruesome ends to the story. Note down several suggestions.

- Start to model the first few lines. Ask pupils to suggest some suitable adjectives to describe the character and the crime. Remind them about rhythm and rhyme by referring back to the model texts. Think about appropriate rhyming words, e.g. *tummy ache/cake.*

Group activities: differentiation

PCM 40

Working in pairs, pupils start to compose their own cautionary tale. They can use the planning/writing frame on **PCM 40** for support.
Lower attainers could continue with the poem begun in shared writing.

Guided writing. Help pupils to run through the alphabet systematically as they search for rhymes, using consonant blends as well as initial letters, and looking for second syllable rhymes where necessary.

Plenary

Comment particularly on the rhyming couplets and regular rhythm. Revise work together. If you have a rhyming dictionary, introduce it now.

EXTENDED WRITING

Pupils finish drafting their cautionary tales, reading and revising them in light of the plenary. They then write a final version for display.

YOU WILL NEED

- **OHT 22** – Henry King
- **OHT 23** – Planning frame
- **PCM 40** – Planning frame

 ICT For activities linked to this lesson see **PAGE 105**

 WATCH OUT FOR

► Difficulty in hearing rhymes and in maintaining regular rhythm.

● NOTEMAKING

MAIN WRITING OBJECTIVES

● **To make short notes by abbreviating ideas and selecting key words.**   4.2 T21
● **To fill out brief notes into connected prose.**   4.2 T22

Word and sentence level objective

● To recognise how commas, connectives and full stops are used to join and separate clauses.   4.2 S4

LESSON ONE

YOU WILL NEED
● **Pupil's Book** page 40
● **OHT 24** – Robbers of the High Seas
● **PCM 41** – Life on Board
● **PCM 42** – Homework

MODEL TEXT

● Explain the lesson objective: *to scan and mark an extract, noting key words, phrases and headings.*

● Show pupils the title of the OHT. Can they predict what it is about?

● Read the first section 'Pirates' aloud, then look at the markings on the text. What do they show? *key words and phrases, paragraph headings*

● What information do the key words in this section give? *what pirates did, when and why*

● With pupils scan the next section to find information about pirate ships. *stolen; small; fast; had cannon and guns*

● Read aloud 'The crew' and mark the text as you talk about it.
  – What are the key words and phrases in the first four sentences? *mixed bunch, criminals, sailors, some were women*
  – What sub-heading could you give to the final paragraph? *rewards*

PB ● Read the text in the Pupil's Book in preparation for group work.

Word and sentence level work

OHT 24 1 Read through the text aloud, emphasising the commas. e.g. *Ever since ships have carried cargo, pirates have attacked them to steal.* Which is the main clause in this sentence? *second part* Why is the first part there? *gives more information*

2 Look at other sentences in which clauses are joined by connectives, e.g. *Some were criminals who had run away to sea.*
Scan the text to find other words that connect two clauses.

ICT For activities linked to this lesson see **PAGE 105**

Group activities: differentiation

PCM 41 **Lower attainers** complete the activities on **PCM 41**. **Higher attainers** complete questions 2 and 3.

Guided reading. Help pupils to pick out important information using key words.

Plenary

Pupils share and discuss their key words from 'Life on Board'. Invite pupils to read aloud their questions. Can others give key words as answers?

Link to reading objectives

- To scan texts to locate key words or phrases.   4.2 T17
- To mark extracts by annotating and by selecting or noting key headings, words or sentences.   4.2 T18

Assumed prior knowledge

- To identify key words, phrases or sentences in reading; to explore ways of writing messages in shortened form.   3.2 T17
- To summarise content of a passage.   3.3 T19
- To identify the features of non-fiction texts.   4.1 T17

Planning suggestion

This unit can be used as part of a week researching, notemaking and writing a report on a topic linked to work in other subjects.

LESSON TWO

SHARED WRITING

- Spend a short time listening to pupils' homework. Did they use all the key words? Did they use commas?

- Explain the lesson objective: *to make notes on aspects of a class topic and use them to write a report.*

OHT 25

- With pupils choose the main heading for the topic. Ask them what aspects of the topic they could include in their report. Encourage them to suggest sub-headings. Note all the suggestions.

- Choose one sub-heading and brainstorm what pupils know about it. Remind them to think of key words and phrases. Note them under the 'What I know' section.

- Decide what other information you will need and list it in the form of questions under the 'What I need to know' section.

- Invite groups of pupils to scan the information books to pick out key words that answer these questions. Note these under 'What I found out'. Note the source of you information on the OHT.

- With pupils' help, use some of the key words under the 'What we know' section to draft a couple of sentences. Model how to add in words of your own to build the notes into sentences.

- Allocate the other sub-headings to groups of pupils to research.

Group activities: differentiation

Pupils should work in groups, using texts at appropriate levels. Encourage pupils to scan rather than read texts to pick out the key words. Pupils make notes and then write sentences relating to their sub-heading.

PCM 43

Lower attainers can use **PCM 43** for support.

Guided writing. Work collaboratively with **lower attainers** helping them to ask questions, find answers and make notes.

Plenary

Invite two or three groups of pupils to talk from their notes about what they have learned. Others comment on how clear the information is.

EXTENDED WRITING

Working on their own, pupils use their notes to draft one or two paragraphs under their heading. You can then paste the pieces into a class poster about the topic.

YOU WILL NEED

- Information books on a class topic suitable for a range of reading abilities
- **OHT 25** – Planning frame
- **PCM 43** – Planning frame
- **Prompt Chart 5** – Information texts

ICT For activities linked to this lesson see **PAGE 105**

WATCH OUT FOR

▶ Repetitive sentences based on each key-word.
▶ Poor links between sentences.

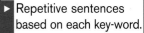

● STORIES FOR YOUNGER CHILDREN

MAIN WRITING OBJECTIVE

- To collaborate with others to write stories with particular audiences in mind. 4.2 T12

Word and sentence level objective

- To use the apostrophe accurately to mark possession. 4.2 S2

LESSON ONE

YOU WILL NEED

- **Pupil's Book** page 42
- **OHT 26** – Mrs Wobble the Waitress
- **PCM 44** – Mr Creep the Crook

MODEL TEXT

- Explain the lesson objective: *to look at examples of stories written for younger children.*

- Ask pupils to think about the books they enjoyed reading when they were younger. Do they remember the Happy Family series by Allan Ahlberg? The books were about characters with alliterative names: Mr Creep the Crook, Miss Jump the Jockey etc.

- Look at the title of the story. Discuss the alliterative name. Ask pupils what they imagine Mrs Wobble will be like. How might the name Wobble fit the job?

- Read the extract aloud. What makes this story suitable for younger children? Highlight some of the features on the OHT. *short sentences, simple words and phrases, familiar story language (One day . . .), repetition, humour, pictures on every page*

- Why is this language easier for young children? *simple words are easy to read, repetition helps you remember things and predict things*

- Mrs Wobble is a bit of a disaster, but at the end of the story she makes her fortune by becoming a performing, wobbling waitress. All the books in the series end happily and most of them are funny. Why do you think this is? *young children might get upset if it doesn't end happily*

Word and sentence level work

1 Does anyone know what the comma in the air in 'a customer's head' is called? What is it for? *an apostrophe, to show the head belongs to the customer*

2 When else are apostrophes used? *to show that a letter is missed out*

Group activities: differentiation

All pupils read the extract on **PCM 44** and underline the repeated words and phrases. They then make notes about how the story might end. **Higher attainers** also pick out the features that make the book suitable for younger children.

ICT For activities linked to this lesson see **PAGE 106**

Plenary

Invite pupils to say what they think will happen at the end of the story and why. Why is this book suitable for younger children?

HOMEWORK

Ask pupils to make up some more characters with suitable alliterative names.

Link to reading objective

- To recognise how certain types of texts are targeted at particular readers; to identify intended audience.   4.2 T9

Assumed prior knowledge

- Sustained story writing, using narrative, characterisation, settings, dialogue.   2.3 T10
- Characters.   4.1 T2
- Alliteration.

Planning suggestion

This Unit can be used as part of a week or more exploring stories written for a particular audience. Pupils' work can be polished and brought to presentational standard. If possible, arrange for the pupils to read their stories to a younger class.

LESSON TWO

SHARED WRITING

- Explain the lesson objective: *to write a story for younger children, for the Happy Families series.*

- Using the **Prompt Chart**, recap the features of stories for younger children.

- Note down some of characters pupils thought of for homework. Comment on which ones are particularly good and why. Take a vote on the favourite and use this as the basis for shared writing.

- Brainstorm some ideas for characters, a simple setting, storyline and ending. Demonstrate how to make notes on the planning sheet.

- With pupils, begin to write the opening sentences. Demonstrate using short, simple sentences. Discuss how you could use repeating phrases. Demonstrate leaving space for pictures.

- Talk about how you might illustrate this opening text to help younger children understand it.

Group activities: differentiation

Working in pairs, pupils plan and begin to draft their own Happy Families story about one of the characters invented for homework. **Lower attainers** can continue with the story from shared writing. **PCM 45** is provided to support planning where necessary.

Guided writing. Emphasise the importance of planning, and help pupils to plan before writing the story.

EXTENDED WRITING

Pupils finish drafting their stories and write them out in a small book leaving space for pictures. They then illustrate it and design a cover.

YOU WILL NEED

- **Prompt Chart 7** – Stories for younger children
- **OHT 27** – Story planner
- **PCM 45** – Story planner
- Flipchart

 ICT For activities linked to this lesson see **PAGE 106**

 WATCH OUT FOR
- ▶ Confusing plot.
- ▶ Over-complicated language.
- ▶ Insufficient planning.

Talking to Rod Theodorou
● NOTEMAKING

MAIN WRITING OBJECTIVES

- **To make short notes, e.g. by abbreviating ideas, selecting key words, listing or in diagrammatic form.**   4.2 T21
- **To fill out brief notes into connected prose.**   4.2 T22

Word and sentence level objective

- To understand the significance of word order.   4.2 S3

LESSON ONE

MODEL TEXT

- Explain the lesson objective: *to find out about how information books are written.*

PB
- Rod Theodorou has written several books. In this interview he explains how he works.

- Spend a few moments brainstorming some questions the pupils would like to ask. Read the interview aloud, maybe asking a pupil to read the questions.

- Ask pupils to explain the difference between planting a garden and building a house. Can they say in their own words why the difference is like writing fiction and non-fiction?

- Why does Rod Theodorou look at lots of different sources? *to see if they agree* Speculate about what you might do if facts don't agree.

- Why do you think he makes notes? *to keep a record of the key facts*

- Where else might you find things out? *other people, leaflets, organisations, TV*

- Why does an information book need a glossary? *to explain new or difficult words*

Word and sentence level work

PB
Look at the questions asked in the interview. Play around with the order of the words, e.g. 'Before you begin to write a book, do you have to know a lot about the subject?'. Discuss how this effects the clarity of the question.

Group activities: differentiation

Working in pairs, pupils brainstorm all the possible sources for finding out facts for an information book on animals. **Higher attainers** then note three key points to remember about writing an information book.

Guided reading. Remind **lower attainers** to use key words only when writing notes.

Plenary

Discuss the sources pupils thought of. Add to the list with ideas such as the RSPCA, Blue Cross, zoos, vets. Then vote and agree on three key points and write them on the board.

YOU WILL NEED

- **Pupil's Book** page 44

 For activities linked to this lesson see **PAGE 106**

HOMEWORK

What makes a good information book? Ask pupils to list three things they think are important e.g. good pictures, diagrams, helpful headings. Then make notes about a really good information book they have read. It doesn't matter if they can't remember the exact title or author.

Link to reading objective

- To appraise a non-fiction book for its contents and usefulness by scanning headings, contents list etc.   4.2 T15

Assumed prior knowledge

- Recording information.   3.1 T22
- Book reviews.   3.3 T14
- Basic understanding of diagrams.

Planning suggestion

This unit is linked to Unit 19 and can be used as part of a week looking at non-fiction texts in detail.

LESSON TWO

SHARED WRITING

- Explain the lesson objective: *to look at some information books and make notes about them.*

- Share ideas from homework. What was good about the books the pupils remember? Brainstorm some of the important features and jot down notes. *clarity, good pictures/diagrams, helpful headings, up-to-date facts etc.*

- Display the book you have chosen to evaluate with the class. Discuss a few details such as the author, publication date, contents, index, etc.

- What questions do you think the book could answer?

- Does the cover make you want to read the book?

- **OHT 28** — Display the evaluation sheet and explain that pupils are going to use this form in their group work.
  Discuss as necessary, including:
  – Why is the publication date important? *to check whether the information is up-to-date*
  – How will you find out what the authors' sources were? *acknowledgements*

- Then look at the book in more detail and together start to fill in the evaluation form. Demonstrate writing in note form.

Group activities: differentiation

PCM 46 — Working in pairs, all pupils evaluate an information book. Each pair will need a copy of **PCM 46**. Each pair then compares their book with another pair and chooses the best, giving reasons. **Lower attainers** do not need to use the **PCM**. Instead they discuss with a partner 3 good things and 3 bad things.

Guided writing. Work with **lower attainers** to evaluate the books orally. Demonstrate how to fill in the form on **PCM 46** using note form.

Plenary

Ask pairs to present their first choice and explain briefly why.

EXTENDED WRITING

Pupils use their notes to write a review of their favourite information book.

YOU WILL NEED

- An information book to look at during shared writing (ideally a big book)
- A range of simple information books for each group
- **OHT 28** – Evaluation sheet
- **PCM 46** – Evaluation sheet

ICT For activities linked to this lesson see **PAGE 106**

WATCH OUT FOR
▶ Difficulty with note form.

73

19 Snake and Lizard

● FACT FILE

MAIN WRITING OBJECTIVE

- **To collect information from a variety of sources and present it in one simple format.** 4.2 T23

Word and sentence level objective

- To examine comparative and superlative adjectives. 4.2 S1

LESSON ONE

YOU WILL NEED
- **Pupil's Book** pages 46–47
- Collection of books on animals
- **PCM 47** – Research planner
- **PCM 48** – Fact file frame

MODEL TEXT

- Explain the lesson objective: *to look at the features of a fact file.*

- Remind pupils of the features of information books.

- **PB** Look at the 'fact file' spread from *Snake and Lizard* by Rod Theodorou. Discuss the meaning of the title 'fact file'. *a set of records, simple short facts and figures – compare with a computer database*

- Look at the layout – what words are in bold print? *headings and subheadings* Point out the varying size of font – the title is the biggest and boldest. How do these features make it easy to read? *break text up into short bits, the headings tell you what each bit is about*

- Introduce the term 'caption' and read them together.

- Ask pupils to recall the interview with Rod Theodorou. Where do pupils think he might have found these facts? *Internet or other books*

Word and sentence level work

PB
1 Ask pupils to identify the adjectives ending -est. *fastest, smallest*

2 Ask pupils how the adjective might end if they were comparing something, e.g. a snake is 'long **-er**' than a worm.

ICT For activities linked to this lesson see **PAGE 106**

Group activities: differentiation

Working in pairs, with access to books, pupils fill in **PCM 47** in order to make a fact file. **Lower attainers** could share a planner, and work on the same animal.

Plenary

Discuss pupils' ideas. Make a list of some of their questions. Check that these are more or less covered by the subheadings on **PCM 48**.

HOMEWORK

Ask pupils to begin to make notes for their own fact file on **PCM 48**. Remind them to note their source materials. You might need to organise loans of useful books or CD-ROMs for homework research.

Link to reading objectives

- To prepare for factual research by reviewing what is known, what is needed, what is available and where one might search.   4.2 T16
- To mark extracts by annotating and by selecting key headings, words or sentences.   4.2 T18

Assumed prior knowledge

- Recording information.   3.1 T22
- Notemaking.   3.2 T17
- Unit 18 Talking to Rod Theodorou

Planning suggestion

This Unit extends the work from Unit 18.

LESSON TWO

SHARED WRITING

- Explain the lesson objective: *to write a Fact file page for a non-fiction book about animals.*

- Explain that all the Fact files should be one side of A4 so that you can make them into a class book.

- Discuss the ideas that pupils had for homework. It may have been difficult to find out some facts and you may need to suggest that sub-headings are adjusted.

- Start to draft a model fact file on the flipchart or OHT. Base it on an animal you know enough about e.g. a rabbit.

- Model how to look for missing facts in an information book using the contents, index, headings etc.

- Discuss ideas for an interesting illustration. Will it be a photo, picture or diagram? Compose a caption, using, 'This …'.

- Make it clear that pupils don't have to use the frame but can compose their own sub-headings if they want to.

Group activities: differentiation

Pupils work in pairs to research and draft animal Fact files. They can use the Fact file writing frame on **PCM 48** if needed. **Lower attainers** can continue with the animal used in shared writing.

Guided writing. Help pupils to keep sentences short, to compose helpful sub-headings, and to find or draw a suitable illustration.

Plenary

Look at work in progress. Discuss suitable lettering and layout. What else will the book need? *index, contents, glossary, cover*

EXTENDED WRITING

Pupils finish writing their Fact files, then plan and design a layout for the final version thinking about size of lettering etc. The files can be compiled into a class information book.

YOU WILL NEED

- Books on a variety of animal topics
- Flipchart or OHT with headings from **PCM 48**
- **PCM 48** – Fact file frame

PCM 48

ICT   For activities linked to this lesson see **PAGE 106**

WATCH OUT FOR

▶ Difficulty in selecting key facts.
▶ Difficulty in using organisational devices.

● SIMILES

MAIN WRITING OBJECTIVE

- **To write own examples of descriptive expressive language based on those read; link to work on adjectives and similes.** 4.2 T13

Word and sentence level objective

- To revise and extend work on adjectives and link to work on figurative language. 4.2 S1

LESSON ONE

MODEL TEXT

- Explain the lesson objective: *to look at poems which describe things using similes.*

- A simile compares one thing with another. It helps to make the meaning clear because the reader can picture the image.

- Give some examples, and invent some together e.g. *as thin as a rake, as hard as nails, as light as a feather*

- Read aloud ' The Writer of this Poem'. Ask pupils:
  – Who is the poem describing? *the poet, Roger McGough*
  – Why doesn't he just say 'I'? *it makes it humorous* Do you think he's really like all these things?
  – What is the first simile in the poem? *taller than a tree*

- Ask pupils to think of a simile for 'handsome as'. Push them to add more detail to cliches such as 'a pop star'.

- Underline the other similes in the poem. Discuss each one, e.g. What is bold about a boxing glove? What is clever about a tick? What do you imagine when you think of a chemist's shop?

Word and sentence level work

Ask pupils to identify the adjectives in the poem. How do these help to create the image? Brainstorm some other adjectives you could use. Look at how they change the image, e.g. 'as cold as the North wind'.

Group activities: differentiation

Working in pairs, pupils read the second poem in their books and complete the sentences on **PCM 49**. **Higher attainers** write similes to describe other colours.

Guided reading. You could read Roger McGough's poem again with **lower attainers**, helping them to pick out adjectives.

Plenary

Discuss some of the similes in the poem: why is red like a trumpet sound? Share some of the similes pupils have invented.

YOU WILL NEED

- **Pupil's Book** page 48
- **OHT 29** – The Writer of this Poem
- **PCM 49** – I asked a little boy
- **PCM 50** – Similes

 ICT For activities linked to this lesson see **PAGE 106**

HOMEWORK

Ask pupils to alter the similes on **PCM 50** by changing the nouns.

Planning suggestion

This unit can be used as part of a week looking at expressive language in poetry, perhaps linking to Units 27 and 29.

LESSON TWO

SHARED WRITING

- Discuss the homework and list some of the new similes.
- Explain the lesson objective: *to write a poem like Roger McGough's, using similes.*
- Explain that you will be focusing on writing similes, so there's no need to try and make it rhyme as well – that would be too difficult.
- Use yourself as the subject for shared writing. Choose one of the adjectives from the OHT, then brainstorm some ideas for the first simile. Encourage children to think of really descriptive adjectives and nouns. Remind them about 'seeing' the image in their heads.
- Ask pupils to suggest other similes.
- Record as many as you can then discuss which works best.

- Using the writing frame, begin to fill in the poem.
- Read the poem aloud as you write. Does it sound right? What could you change?

Group activities: differentiation

Pupils compose their own simile poems using 'The writer of this poem' as a model. They can use the writing frame on **PCM 51** if they wish. Encourage them to change the adjectives if they need to.

Lower attainers can continue with the poem from shared writing.

Guided writing. Write alongside one group. Read the poem aloud as you work and ask for feedback.

Plenary

Read out work in progress and evaluate. How vivid are the descriptions? Could the similes be improved?

EXTENDED WRITING

Pupils revise their poems and write out a final copy. Pupils who can cope with the challenge could try to revise their poems into a rhyming version.

YOU WILL NEED

- Flipchart
- **OHT 30** – Writing frame
- **PCM 51** – Writing frame
- **Prompt Chart 4** – Writing poetry

ICT For activities linked to this lesson see **PAGE 106**

WATCH OUT FOR

- ▶ Cliches.
- ▶ Poor understanding of similes.

21

The Scrapyard of the Future

PRESENTING INFORMATION

MAIN WRITING OBJECTIVE

- **To collect information from a variety of sources and present it in one simple format.**   4.2 T23

Word and sentence level objective

- To use alternative words which are more accurate.   4.2 W9

LESSON ONE

YOU WILL NEED

- **Pupils' Book** pages 50-51

MODEL TEXT

- Explain the lesson objective: *to get information from a chart and a labelled diagram.*

- Remind pupils of times when they have used charts or diagrams to present information, e.g. in science, geography or mathematics.

PB

- Ask pupils to scan the information in their books to get a general idea of how it is organised. What are the extracts about?

- Read the introduction and the text for Station 1. Ask pupils:
  – What liquids, other than oil are removed at Station 1? *petrol, water, brake fluid*
  – What extra infomation does the illustration give? *shape of the tank, how oil gets to tank*

- Invite pupils to pick out the next five headings and read the text. Ask them to pick out the key words at Station 4. *glass, cut, windscreen, separate* And Station 6. *body, smashed*

- Now look at the chart. What is the heading? What are the sub-headings?

- Show pupils how to interpret it. Why is the information presented in this way? *easy to get key information quickly*

Word and sentence level work

PB

1 Scan the text for verbs, e.g. *screwed, smashed, cut.*

2 Ask pupils to think of alternatives with similar meanings. Would these be more or less effective in the context?

Group activities: Differentiation

Pupils scan the text for information. All pupils complete questions 1 and 2. **Higher attainers** can go on to questions 3 and 4.

Plenary

Ask pupils to summarise the extract. Who is most accurate? How did the pictures help?

How long do pupils think it takes to take a car apart? Ask them to justify their opinions.

ICT For activities linked to this lesson see **PAGE 106**

HOMEWORK

Ask pupils to skim through magazines or newspapers to find different or unusual ways of presenting information, e.g. lists, charts, diagrams, pictures.

Link to reading objectives

- To scan texts to locate key words or phrases, useful headings and key sentences, and use these to summarise a text.   4.2 T17
- To mark extracts by annotating and by selecting key headings, words or sentences.   4.2 T18

Assumed prior knowledge

- To be able to write simple non-chronological reports.   3.1 T23
- To write non-fiction texts using headings, captions etc.   2.3 T20
- To summarise orally the content of a passage or text.   3.3 T19

Planning suggestion

The focus of the week could be collecting and presenting information. Link the work to a class topic. It would be useful to have a range of charts relating to different subjects – e.g. mathematics, science, geography – to start discussions.

LESSON TWO

SHARED WRITING

- Spend a few minutes looking at the different ways of presenting information that pupils have found. Why is the information presented in that particular way? Point out that some information has hardly any words, e.g. a weather map or instructions.

- Explain the lesson objective: *to make a class wall-chart giving information about work they have been doing in another subject, e.g. the Victorians: clothes, school, travel.*

- Select one aspect of the topic and brainstorm what pupils know about it. Show how to select and highlight key information.

- Group the information under sub-headings, listing which facts will go under which heading.

- Discuss how the information could best be presented, *e.g. spider diagram, map, chart, using boxes, colour coding etc.* Do you need diagrams or illustrations? Choose the most effective form of presentation for the subject matter, making sure pupils understand the reasons for the choice.

- Allocate a different part of the chart (a sub-heading) to each group.

Group activities: Differentiation

Pupils work in mixed ability groups to make notes from information books and draft a section of the chart.

Guided writing. Help **lower attainers** to pick out key words from information sources. Discuss how they are going to present their information and why.

Plenary

Ask pupils to read their notes and say where they found the information. Discuss how they intend to present it and why. Will their work fit on the chart?

EXTENDED WRITING

Groups should finish drafting their section of the chart, then swap their piece with another group. Is it clear? They then present a final version, including any drawings or diagrams, for the class wall-chart.

YOU WILL NEED

- Examples of different ways of presenting information (collected by pupils and yourself)
- Blank flipchart or OHT
- Books and other information about a class topic
- **Prompt Chart 5** – Information texts

ICT For activities linked to this lesson see **PAGE 106**

WATCH OUT FOR

▶ Over-long sentences.
▶ Irrelevant detail.
▶ Uneccessary pictures.

22

Jason and the School Bully 1

● SOCIAL ISSUES

MAIN WRITING OBJECTIVE

- **To explore the main issues of a story by writing a story about a dilemma and the issues it raises for the character.**   4.3 T11

Word and sentence level objective

- To identify common punctuation marks, including commas and speech marks.   4.3 S2

LESSON ONE

YOU WILL NEED

- **Pupil's Book** pages 53–54
- **PCM 52** – Motivations

MODEL TEXT

- Explain the lesson objective: *to look at how different characters in a story behave when faced with a dilemma.*

- Read the extract aloud. Ask pupils:
  – Which of the boys is the bully? How do they know? *Craig, because he picks on Jason, teases him etc.*
  – How does Alistair feel about Craig? What words tell us? *he's afraid – 'trying not to give Craig an excuse to pick on him', 'giggling nervously'*
  – Is Jason scared of Craig? *doesn't seem to be*
  – How do we know? *'Can't you get it repaired?', 'Sullivan the skunk'*

- Discuss how the boys react differently to the bully. What does Alistair do? What does Craig do? What makes Alistair behave the way he does?

- How do you feel about Alistair?

Word and sentence level work

1 Ask pupils to identify the commas in the first few lines of text. Read these lines aloud together, pausing after each comma. Now show them what the piece would sound like if commas were ignored.

2 Ask them to imagine the text without speech marks. Would they know when someone was speaking? What do they notice about the changes?

Group activities: Differentiation

Lower attainers complete the activity on **PCM 52**. **Higher attainers** complete questions 2 and 3.

Guided reading. Read through the text with **lower attainers** and discuss how the characters behave and why.

Plenary

What was Alistair's problem at the beginning? How did he deal with it? Why does Jason behave the way he does?

ICT   For activities linked to this lesson see **PAGE 107**

HOMEWORK

Ask pupils to think about what might happen next in the story. What will Jason do?

Link to reading objective

- To identify social, moral or cultural issues in stories, e.g. the dilemmas faced by characters, and to discuss how the characters deal with them. 4.3 T1

Assumed prior knowledge

- Typical story themes. 3.2 T2
- To understand how characters are built up and how readers respond to them. 4.1 T1
- To identify the main characteristics of key characters, drawing on the text. 4.1 T2

Planning suggestion

The focus of the week's work could be on the problems faced by characters in different stories. Discussions based on some of these issues should prepare pupils for writing an extended story based on a dilemma (Unit 23).

LESSON TWO

SHARED WRITING

- Explain the lesson objective: *to continue writing the story of* Jason and the School Bully, *using some of their homework ideas.*

- Recap what happened in the story. With pupils brainstorm what might happen next. Refer pupils to the opening lines of the chapter 'Jason's Last Defeat Ever' – what clues does this give you?

  - What might Craig do next? *he could get even more unpleasant, he could turn on Alistair*
  - What options did Alistair have? *he could keep teasing Jason, he could decide to support his friend*
  - What might Jason do? *he might get angry with Craig and stand up to him, he might try and walk away*

- Choose one of the ideas to develop. Ask pupils to suggest the sequence of events. What will happen? Will someone get hurt? Will they get into trouble? Will someone else come along? How will it end?

- Using pupils' suggestions write the next paragraph of the story. Encourage them to suggest some suitable dialogue. Model the use of commas before or after speech, and within the text.

- Discuss how the characters might be feeling. What words could you use to show this?

Group activities: Differentiation

All pupils write a continuation of the story. **Lower attainers** can use the notes from shared writing. **Higher attainers** should be encouraged to develop their own ideas, using **PCM 53** to help their planning.

Guided writing. Help **lower attainers** to write paragraphs about the main events. Encourage them to show how the characters feel.

Plenary

Invite three pupils to read aloud their work in progress. Comment on words or phrases which emphasise characters' feelings.

EXTENDED WRITING

Pupils finish the first draft of their story, then read it to a partner. Does it show how the characters feel and what they say? They then revise it and write a final version.

YOU WILL NEED

- **Pupil's Book** pages 53–54
- Flipchart or blank OHT
- **PCM 53** – Planning frame
- **Prompt Chart 3** – Descriptive writing

 For activities linked to this lesson see **PAGE 107**

WATCH OUT FOR

- ▶ Lack of understanding of issue.
- ▶ Lack of speech.
- ▶ Few details of how characters feel.

● EXTENDED STORY

MAIN WRITING OBJECTIVE

● **To write own longer stories in chapters from story plans.** 4.3 T13

Word and sentence level objective

● To distinguish the two forms: *its (possessive no apostrophe)* and *it's (contracted 'it is')* and to use these accurately in own writing. 4.3 W10

LESSON ONE

MODEL TEXT

● Recap what has happened in the story so far and discuss some of the pupils' ideas for what happened next.

● Explain the lesson objective: *to find out what happens next and to look at some alternative courses of action.*

● Read aloud the next part of the story. Choose three pupils to read the dialogue. Ask pupils to summarise what happened. *Jason was so angry and upset that he flew into a rage and attacked Craig.*

● Discuss why Jason did this. *he had had enough, he just snapped*

● Do pupils think it was a wise thing to do? Why, or why not?

● Why is the bike described as blurred and fuzzy? *seen through tears*

● How does Craig react? What does he say? *he's angry and upset; he threatens Jason – 'I'll kill you for this. Wait til tomorrow!'*

● What is Jason's dilemma at the end? *He can either go to school and face the bully, or lie to his mum and pretend he is sick.*

Word and sentence level work

Find examples of *its* and *it's* in the text. Ask pupils why one has the apostrophe and the other doesn't. Explain that *it's* is short for *it is*, whilst *its* is used to show possession, e.g. *the bike was on its side.*

Group activities: differentiation

Pupils work in pairs to think of alternative courses of action to those listed on **PCM 54**. **Lower attainers** could do the first two sections only.

Guided reading. Look at the motivation for characters' actions and think about how they might act differently.

Plenary

Look at each of the dilemmas. What other course of action could the characters have taken? Do pupils agree with the writer's solution for each of the problems? Why or why not?

YOU WILL NEED

● **Pupil's Book** page 56
● **PCM 54** – Alternative actions
● **PCM 55** – Homework

 For activities linked to this lesson see **PAGE 107**

HOMEWORK

Pupils work on **PCM 55** writing the correct term; *its* or *it's.*

Link to reading objective

- To write critically about an issue or dilemma raised in a story, explaining the problem, alternative courses of action and evaluating the writer's solution. **4.3 T8**

Assumed prior knowledge

- To identify typical story themes. **3.2 T2**
- To understand how characters are built up and how readers respond to them. **4.1 T1**
- To identify the main characteristics of key characters, drawing on the text. **4.1 T2**

Planning suggestion

This unit provides a continuation of the work in Unit 22, looking at the problems and dilemmas faced by characters. Pupils can plan and write their own extended story based on the week's discussion of bullying as an issue.

LESSON TWO

SHARED WRITING

- Explain the lesson objective: *to write their own longer stories about a dilemma, in chapters, and from story plans.*

- Recap all the work done so far on *Jason and the School Bully*.

- Ask pupils to share dilemmas they have faced. Tell them they can use their own ideas as the basis for a story, but they can change the characters and events.

- Think of a dilemma from your own experience and use this to model planning a story.

- Let pupils suggest what might go into the first chapter or episode. Review the notes to make sure enough detail is provided.

- Make brief notes about what will happen in Chapters 2 and 3. Remind them about the use of 'cliffhanger' endings to make the reader read on.

- Discuss how the story might end.

- With contributions from pupils, begin to write a draft of the first episode or chapter of the story. Include some dialogue.

Group activities: Differentiation

Pupils use **PCM 56** to plan their own story about a dilemma. They should then read and comment on each other's plans. **Higher attainers** should start drafting their stories.

Guided writing. Scribe a group story plan with **lower attainers**. Work on introducing some new action into each chapter.

Plenary

Invite a few pupils to share their plans. Have they made the dilemma clear? Is there a good link between chapters? Is there a good resolution to the story?

EXTENDED WRITING

Pupils draft their stories, following their plans closely. They can swap drafts with a partner for comment, before writing a final version.

YOU WILL NEED

- **OHT 31** – Planning frame
- **PCM 56** – Planning frame
- **Prompt Chart 2** – Planning a story

 ICT For activities linked to this lesson see **PAGE 107**

 WATCH OUT FOR
- Limited use of story plans.
- Lack of continuity between episodes.

MAIN WRITING OBJECTIVE

- **To assemble and sequence points in order to plan the presentation of a point of view.**　　　　4.3 T21

Word and sentence level objectives

- To use a range of presentational skills.　　　　4.3 W15
- The use of connectives to structure an argument.　　　　4.3 S4

LESSON ONE

MODEL TEXT

YOU WILL NEED
- **Pupil's Book** page 58
- **OHT 32** – Point of view

- Explain the lesson objective: *to look at a piece of writing which presents a point of view.*

- Ask pupils to think of situations when they might say 'it's not fair!' e.g. *they might think being made to go outside at break is unfair*

- Take just one issue. Does everyone agree? Explain that there is no right and wrong answer, but that different people hold different points of view. A debate is when people discuss their different points of view.

- Read the extract aloud. Mark the OHT as you discuss:
  – What have this class been debating? *whether they should only allow football in the playground on certain days of the week*
  – What is the writer's point of view? *should be allowed every day*
  – Why does he hold this point of view? *most people like it, it's fun*
  – Why do some people think this isn't fair? *takes up too much space in the playground, people get hurt, can be scary for smaller kids*

- Look at how the writer presents the argument. Paragraph 1 introduces the debate, paragraph 2 states why people think it is unfair, paragraph 3 states the other point of view, and paragraph 4 summarises the writer's point of view and his reasons.

Word and sentence level work

Highlight the use of connectives/connective phrases to link sentences and structure the argument *e.g. They say . . . because; They also say; On the other hand; And if . . .; Also . . .; I think . . . because*

Group activities: differentiation

Pupils decide which point of view they agree with and write down their reasons.

Guided reading. Work with **lower attainers** helping them to understand the arguments and to summarise their point of view.

Plenary

Ask pupils to read out their summaries: *I think . . . because . . .* Take a class vote on which is the most popular point of view.

ICT For activities linked to this lesson see **PAGE 107**

HOMEWORK

Ask pupils to make a list of things that they think are unfair in school. They should also think about their reasons for holding that point of view.

Link to reading objectives

- To read, compare and evaluate examples of arguments and
  discussions.   4.3 T16
- To look at how arguments are presented.   4.3 T17

Assumed prior knowledge

- Connectives.

Planning suggestion

This unit can be used as part of a week looking at structuring an argument and writing persuasively. It can be linked to Unit 28.

LESSON TWO

SHARED WRITING

- Explain the lesson objective: *to write a discussion text putting forward a point of view.*

- Discuss pupils' homework ideas – what they think is not fair and why.

- Recap how Paul put across his point of view about football. He presented both sides of the argument, before stating his own point of view.

- Choose one issue. It should be something about which there is disagreement in the class. Brainstorm points for and against on the flipchart.

- Using the writing frame, begin to model writing a discussion text. Show pupils how to use paragraphs to structure the argument. Model the use of connective phrases, such as *also, because, as a result of, on the other hand*

- Model summarising your own point of view in the last paragraph.

- Ask pupils to think about who they might write this for – another teacher perhaps, or the person in charge of setting the rule they disagree with. Remind them to consider their audience when they write, and that they are trying to persuade the reader to agree with their point of view.

Group activities: differentiation

Working in pairs, pupils choose an issue and make notes of arguments for and against using **PCM 57**. They then write a first draft of their discussion text. **Lower attainers** could continue with the work from shared writing. A writing frame is provided on **PCM 58**.

Guided writing. Help **higher attainers** to use a variety of connectives to structure their argument.

Plenary

Ask pairs to read their scripts or present their arguments.

EXTENDED WRITING

Pupils revise and redraft their texts, then present them in a suitable format to an appropriate audience.

YOU WILL NEED

- Flipchart with headings *For* and *Against*
- **OHT 33** – Writing frame
- **PCM 57** – For and against
- **PCM 58** – Writing frame
- **Prompt Chart 8** – Point of view

For activities linked to this lesson see **PAGE 107**

WATCH OUT FOR
- ► Problems with logical sequencing.
- ► Not presenting both sides of the debate.

It wasn't a brick ...

● ALTERNATIVE ENDINGS

MAIN WRITING OBJECTIVE

- **To write an alternative ending for a known story.** 4.3 T12

Word and sentence level objective

- To identify common punctuation marks. 4.3 S2

LESSON ONE

YOU WILL NEED
- **Pupil's Book** page 60
- **PCM 59** – Being Afraid
- **PCM 60** – Homework

MODEL TEXT

- Explain the lesson objective: *to look at a story ending and think about why it ends that way.*

- Introduce the extract by reading the summary. The story is told by a boy called Sausage. Read the extract.

- Ask pupils for their immediate reaction to this ending. Were they excited? Were they disappointed?
  – How did Sausage feel about his find? *a bit disappointed, but it was more important to him that he'd got back to the surface*
  – Why is he going to keep the tin as long as he lives? *he's so proud to have done the dive and conquered his fear*
  – Why does he think he might easily live to be a hundred? *he feels almost superhuman after what he's done*

- Talk about what was important to Sausage. How does this help pupils to see that this is a good ending? *it was more important to Sausage to conquer his fear, than to find any treasure*

Word and sentence level work

1 Look at the punctuation. What are the dashes and the colon for? *dash is a pause before saying more about something – e.g. the tin; a colon is like a dash but more important – it introduces something*

2 Look at the two semi-colons. A semi-colon is a longer pause than a comma, but isn't a full stop. Try changing them to full stops to show how the two halves of the sentence are connected by the semi-colon.

Group activities: differentiation

Working in pairs, pupils read the extract on **PCM 59**, and answer the questions.

Guided reading. Read the extract through with **lower attainers**. How did Sausage feel under the water? How does this help to explain why he kept the tin?

Plenary

Ask pupils to feedback their views of the ending now they've read more about Sausage. How would it alter the story if Sausage had found a fortune? Or if he hadn't managed to dive at all?

ICT For activities linked to this lesson see **PAGE 107**

HOMEWORK

Ask pupils to choose an alternative ending for the story and make notes on **PCM 60**. **Lower attainers** should look at option 1; **Higher attainers** should look at option 2.

Link to reading objectives

- To identify dilemmas faced by characters and how the characters deal with them.   4.3 T1
- To explain alternative courses of action.   4.3 T8

Assumed prior knowledge

- To identify and map out the main stages of a story.   4.1 T4
- Character.   4.1 T2

Planning suggestion

This unit can be used as part of a week looking at story endings. You could explore the endings of some more familiar stories, such as fairy tales. This unit can also be used to explore dilemma in more detail, linked to Units 22 and 23.

LESSON TWO

SHARED WRITING

- Explain the lesson objective: *to write an alternative ending to* Return to Air *(two paragraphs).*

- Recap what happened at the end of the story. Ask pupils to suggest some alternative endings. Discuss why these may or may not be suitable alternatives. Remind them that they are only writing another couple of paragraphs and that they are writing a story ENDING so they can't introduce a whole new plot line.

- Choose the most obvious alternative – probably that Sausage finds something *in* the tin. Discuss what it might be – old coins, old letters, a ring.

- Why would old coins be a good idea? *we know that Sausage collects coins*

- Using the frame, and pupils' ideas, start to write a description of the discovery. Then discuss how it could have got there.

- Make notes for what might happen in paragraph 2. Discuss what Sausage might do with his find. Ask pupils to suggest words that describe his feelings.

- Briefly discuss how you could round the story off.

Group activities: differentiation

In pairs, pupils draft an alternative ending (two paragraphs). **Lower attainers** may continue with the version started in shared writing, or use the writing frame on **PCM 61.**

Guided writing. Help pupils to round the story off satisfactorily.

Plenary

Listen to some of the endings. Discuss how some of the alternatives would fit a different kind of story. Maybe Sausage faces a different dilemma – needs money, trying to prove himself to a friend etc.

EXTENDED WRITING

Pupils should write a different beginning which better fits their alternative ending.

YOU WILL NEED

- **OHT 34** – Writing frame
- **PCM 61** – Writing frame

For activities linked to this lesson see
PAGE 107

WATCH OUT FOR

▸ Introducing new themes.
▸ Failure to find a suitable line to end on.

MAIN WRITING OBJECTIVE

- **To design an advertisement.**   4.3 T25

Word and sentence level objectives

- To understand how the grammar of a sentence alters when the sentence type is altered.   4.3 S3
- Compound words.   4.3 W11
- To use a range of presentational skills.   4.3 W15

LESSON ONE

MODEL TEXT

YOU WILL NEED
- **Pupil's Book** pages 62–63
- **PCM 62** – Children's adverts
- **Prompt Chart 9** – Persuasive features of adverts

- Explain the lesson objective: *to look at some advertisements and discuss how persuasive they are.*

- Look at the advertisements together:
  - How do these adverts grab our attention? *big lettering, bright colours, pictures*
  - How do they try to persuade us? *special offers, free gifts, new and better products, big promises*
  - What is the second advert trying to persuade us to buy? *The Dandy* (If children say 'Fungums' explain why they are wrong, and discuss what this ad is doing.)

- Look at the persuasive language of the adverts.
  - Discuss why the first advert says '4 days only'? *makes you go and buy things straight away in case you miss out on the offers*
  - What words make the pupils interested in the second advert? *free next week, given away, (maybe) fungums*
  - Why is the third advert is successful? *humour; bright colours; special offer*

- Can anyone point out examples of alliteration? *fascinating facts … favourite football stars*

Word and sentence level work

1 Ask pupils to find examples of compound words, e.g. *weekend, newsagent, clearout* Unpick their meaning.

2 Ask pupils to pick out phrases that are not sentences, e.g. *Bikes for kids of all ages; Given away with The Dandy* Rewrite them as proper sentences. Discuss the effect this has.

Group activities: differentiation

Working in pairs, all pupils evaluate the advertisements on **PCM 62** and suggest improvements. They could also annotate to show the different persuasive techniques. **Lower attainers** could look at one advert only.

Plenary

Ask pupils to feedback their evaluation of the adverts. Make a list of all the persuasive features noticed. Discuss suggested revisions.

ICT For activities linked to this lesson see **PAGE 108**

HOMEWORK

Ask pupils to look for examples of fun, catchy adverts in magazines and newspapers.

- To evaluate advertisements for their impact.   4.3 T19

Assumed prior knowledge

- Knowledge of a range of presentational devices, e.g. enlarged print, captions, headings etc.   3.1 S9
- Alliteration.

Planning suggestion

This unit can be used as part of a week looking at persuasive language in a variety of forms: posters, advertisements, letters. It can be linked to Unit 28.

LESSON TWO

SHARED WRITING

- Look at some examples of adverts collected for homework. Evaluate them against the features on the **Prompt Chart**.

- Explain the lesson objective: *to advertise ourselves!*

- Discuss some of the qualities they might want to emphasise, or things about themselves they could 'sell' e.g. *very helpful round the house, useful babysitter, good at sport, clever*

- Start to work on the language – the use of exciting phrases, compound words and alliteration, e.g. *spectacular science student; brilliant babysitter; megabrain with the mostest.*

- Recap the key features to remember.

- Model an advert for yourself. Brainstorm a main heading, e.g *Top Teacher*

- Ask pupils to suggest phrases you could use to 'sell' yourself. Can they think of a 'special offer'? *World's best teacher will teach you for free!* Begin to sketch out the headings and the text.

Group activities: differentiation

Pupils work in pairs to brainstorm ideas, words and phrases for advertising themselves. They then produce their own individual rough draft. **Lower attainers** can continue with the example from shared writing using **PCM 63**.

Guided writing. Continue writing your own advert alongside one group. Model response partner work by discussing it with the group and asking them to help you to improve it.

Plenary

Look at work in progress and evaluate against the features on the **Prompt Chart**. How persuasive are the adverts?

EXTENDED WRITING

Pupils revise and polish their ads, then make a final copy, spacing lettering carefully and using a variety of print and capital letters.

YOU WILL NEED

- **OHT 35** – Advert writing frame
- **PCM 63** – Advert writing frame
- **Prompt Chart 9** – Persuasive features of adverts

ICT For activities linked to this lesson see **PAGE 108**

WATCH OUT FOR !
- ▶ Difficulty with presentation and layout.

MAIN WRITING OBJECTIVES

- To write poems, experimenting with different styles and structures. 4.3 T14
- To produce polished poetry through revision. 4.3 T15

Word and sentence level objective

- To understand that some words can be changed and others cannot, e.g. changing verb endings. 4.3 S1

LESSON ONE

MODEL TEXT

- Explain the lesson objective: *to look at ways of patterning poems without using rhyme.*

- Introduce the poet, James Berry. He comes from Jamaica but now lives in England. Read 'Childhood Tracks', emphasising the repeated verbs.
  – What clues are there that the poem isn't set in this country? *jelly-coconut, village-made wet sugar, calabash gourd, fermenting pineapples, palm trees, hot climate*

- Look at the first three verses in detail.

- Highlight words and phrases which convey the heat and peacefulness of the scene. Discuss the stillness and slowness of life in very hot weather.

- Ask pupils to find the pattern of the poem. *repeated verbs, -ing endings, describing sense*

- Look at the rhythm of the lines. There is no rhyme. Introduce the term **verse**. These verses vary in length. Look at where the divisions come.

- Ask pupils to find examples of alliteration. *fried fish, patch of pineapples.* Read the verses aloud again to help them hear the rhythm of the words, and the alliterative sounds.

Word and sentence level work

1 What effect does it have to change the verb ending, e.g. I ate, I drank, I smelt. *these are much harder words, not so rhymical*
Why do you think James Berry chose the -ing ending? *It gives the impression of these things going on over a long time; they have a softer, gentler rhythm.*

2 Look up some of the unfamiliar vocabulary in a good dictionary.

Group activities: differentiation

Working in pairs, pupils use **PCM 64** to make a sense web of the poem. **Lower attainers** could work on just one or two verses. **Higher attainers** should go on to think of their own ideas for 'touching'.

Plenary

Display some of the sense webs. Ask pupils to suggest some touch impressions.

YOU WILL NEED

- **Pupil's Book** page 64
- **OHT 36** – Verses 1–3
- **PCM 64** – Sense web
- **PCM 65** – Homework

 ICT For activities linked to this lesson see **PAGE 108**

HOMEWORK

Ask pupils to focus on their sense impressions during the first half hour after they get home from school. What do they see, hear, taste, smell and touch? They should make notes on **PCM 65**.

Link to reading objectives

- To understand poetic terms and identify: verse, stanza, rhyme, rhythm, alliteration.   4.3 T4
- To discuss how a poet does or does not use rhyme.   4.3 T6

Assumed prior knowledge

- Experience of a range of poetry.
- Adjectives.   3.2 S2/S3
- Alliteration.   3.3 T15

Planning suggestion

This unit could be used as part of a week looking at different forms of poetry, comparing non-rhyming poems such as this to poems with a strong rhyme scheme. This work could be linked to Unit 29.

LESSON TWO

SHARED WRITING

- Explain the lesson objective: *to write their own senses poem.*

- Display one pupil's completed web from group activities and briefly recap detail from James Berry's poem.

- Discuss some of the notes pupils made for homework about what they saw, heard etc when they got home from school.

OHT 37

- Ask pupils to concentrate on what they could hear when they got home from school. Make notes. Do the same for smell.

- On a flipchart, begin to draft a first verse, encouraging pupils to really try and 'hear' the sound before trying to describe it. Ask them to suggest suitable adjectives.

- Go back and rework each line, crossing out and changing words. With pupils' help, find words which work hard and which conjure up a vivid sense impression.

- Model reading the draft aloud to see how it sounds. Explain that this is a good way of testing the effect of your poetry as you write.

Group activities: differentiation

PCM 66

Pupils work in pairs, sharing ideas but producing individual poems. Remind them to concentrate hard on the sense impressions they noted for homework. They can use the writing frame on **PCM 66** to help them. **Lower attainers** could continue with the work from shared writing. Encourage pupils to read their poems aloud and revise as they write.

Guided writing. Help pupils to select words which vividly describe their sense impressions.

Plenary

Share some of the work in progress. Encourage comments on how to improve individual lines.

EXTENDED WRITING

1 Pupils swap drafts with a partner. They should concentrate on the images. How powerful are they? They then make one or two suggestions for improvement.
2 Pupils then produce a polished version of their own poem for a class anthology of sense poems.

YOU WILL NEED

- **OHT 37** – Planning frame
- Flipchart
- **PCM 66** – Writing frame
- **Prompt Chart 4** – Writing poetry

⚠ WATCH OUT FOR

- ▶ Bland vocabulary.
- ▶ Lack of awareness of senses.
- ▶ Use of 'saw' 'heard' etc.

28 I'm writing to ask …

● PERSUASIVE LETTERS

MAIN WRITING OBJECTIVE

- **To write persuasively in the form of a letter.**   4.3 T23

Word and sentence level objectives

- To use connectives to structure an argument.   4.3 S4
- To use contractions and to distinguish apostrophes used for possession and contraction. (Revise)   4.2 S2

LESSON ONE

MODEL TEXT

- Explain the lesson objective: *to look at letters written to persuade.*

- Read both letters aloud. Ask pupils to say what the purpose of each letter is. Who wrote it? Who were they writing to? Why?

- Compare the different beginnings and endings – why are they so different? Discuss purpose and audience.

- What do you think might persuade Anna's parents to come and 'rescue' her? *praising her mum's cooking; 'I really miss you', 'PLEASE PLEASE'; they may be worried that she is unhappy*

- Do you think her PS will convince them?

- Look at Mrs Lacey's letter. Ask pupils to point out some of the persuasive language she uses. *I think it's very important, I'll make Mark take some work, I do hope you will agree*

- Would the letter make good sense without these phrases? *yes, but it wouldn't sound persuasive*

Word and sentence level work

1 Scan the letters for examples of contractions. *can't, won't, it's, I'm, I'll, he'll*

2 Ask pupils to pick out examples of connectives used to join sentences. *and, because, but* Point out that these are good words to use when presenting an argument or point of view.

Group activities: differentiation

All pupils evaluate Mrs Lacey's argument. **Lower attainers** can use **PCM 67** for support. **Higher attainers** can go on to suggest other reasons she could give to keep Mark off school.

Guided reading. Help **lower attainers** to pick out the persuasive vocabulary.

Plenary

Evaluate Mrs Lacey's argument. Is it effective? Ask **higher attainers** to read out their own arguments.

YOU WILL NEED

- **Pupil's Book** page 66
- **PCM 67** – Mrs Lacey's letter
- **Prompt Chart 10** – Persuasive letters

 ICT For activities linked to this lesson see **PAGE 108**

HOMEWORK

Ask pupils to make a list of subjects they could write a persuasive letter about, and to suggest who they might write to. It could be parents, a friend, or a teacher. Encourage them to think of something they would genuinely want to persuade someone to do.

Link to reading objective

- From examples of persuasive writing, to investigate how style and
  vocabulary are used to convince the reader.   4.3 T18

Assumed prior knowledge

- Letter writing.   3.3 T20/23
- Connectives and complex sentences.   3.3 S5

LESSON TWO

SHARED WRITING

- Explain the lesson objective: *to write a persuasive letter.*

- Brainstorm some subjects and situations. *e.g. asking for more pocket money; later bedtime; wanting a pet; asking to be let off PE; begging a friend to let you borrow a prize possession*

- Choose a subject which is relevant to the whole class. It should be something that pupils feel strongly about. It is much easier to be persuasive if you really want or believe in something.

- Ask pupils to suggest what the main arguments would be. Make notes of some persuasive words and phrases that you could use in the letter.

- Start to draft the letter, modelling the use of polite, persuasive language and connectives such as 'because'. Show pupils how to adapt the writing frame to suit the purpose if necessary.

- Read the argument back as you write. How persuasive is it?

OHT 38

Group activities: differentiation

PCM 68

Working in pairs, pupils draft a persuasive letter. Those who need to can use the writing frame provided on **PCM 68**. **Lower attainers** can continue with the letter started in shared writing.

Guided writing. Help pupils to think of convincing arguments and to set the letter out correctly.

Plenary

Ask pupils to read out their work in progress. How convincing are their letters?

EXTENDED WRITING

Pupils finish drafting their letters and swap with another pair. They then revise and edit, and write out a final version. If possible, encourage them to send the letters to see if they really persuade!

YOU WILL NEED

- **OHT 38** – Letter writing frame
- **PCM 68** – Letter writing frame
- **Prompt Chart 10** – Persuasive letters

ICT For activities linked to this lesson see **PAGE 108**

WATCH OUT FOR

➤ Failure to use correct letter conventions.
➤ Weak arguments.
➤ Impolite tone.

Skipping, Clapping and Counting

● PLAYGROUND RHYMES

MAIN WRITING OBJECTIVE

- **To write poems, experimenting with different styles and structures.**   4.3 T14

Word and sentence level objectives

- Spelling using phonemes.   4.3 W3
- To spell words with common letter strings but different pronunciations. 4.3 W6

LESSON ONE

MODEL TEXT

- Explain the lesson objective: *to look at some playground rhymes.*

- Ask pupils to recite any playground rhymes they know, e.g. for ball-bouncing, skipping, or counting out. What do they have in common? *catchy rhymes and rhythms, easy to remember, repeated chorus, humour*

- Read the rhymes in the Pupil's Book aloud, then repeat them with everyone joining in.

- What do they have in common? *bouncy rhythms, rhymes, repeated phrases, nonsense words, easy to learn*

- Ask pupils how the rhyme works in each poem. *'Skipping': internal rhyme – one and tongue, two and shoe etc; 'Clapping': life/wife; 'Counting': obble/bobble, out/sprout*

- Discuss the kind of actions each rhyme would have to go with it. The middle one is a complicated clapping pattern (a bit like pat-a-cake).

- Why are there so many different versions of playground rhymes? *as they are handed down they get changed slightly at different times and in different places* Share any you remember from childhood.

Word and sentence level work

1 Look again at the rhymes in the skipping rhyme. Can pupils think of a more accurate rhyme for 'twist'? *list, fist, missed, kissed*

2 Look at the different spellings of rhyming sounds, e.g. two/shoe. Ask pupils to think of some more, e.g. *four/floor/more; six/sticks etc*

3 Find examples of words with the same letter strings which *don't* rhyme, e.g. *one/stone; four/hour*

Group activities – differentiation

In pairs, pupils write more verses for the skipping poem, using **PCM 69**. **Lower attainers** could just find rhymes for the numbers (which may or may not be actions) instead of writing out the line.

Plenary

Listen to some of the skipping rhymes. Make a list of the rhymes on the board.

YOU WILL NEED

- **Pupil's Book** pages 68–69
- **PCM 69** – Skipping rhyme

ICT For activities linked to this lesson see **PAGE 108**

HOMEWORK

Pupils can ask their parents, grandparents or other adults/relatives to recite any playground rhymes they can remember from their childhood. They should write them down or try to memorise them.

PB

PB

PCM 69

Planning suggestion

This unit offers an opportunity to spend a week looking at rhyme and rhythm patterns in poetry. Try and involve parents and other relatives, or do some active research in the playground!

LESSON TWO

SHARED WRITING

- Explain the lesson objective: *to write some original playground rhymes for a class collection.*

- Listen to some rhymes that pupils collected for homework. Write some down if possible, to start off the class collection.

- Refer pupils back to the rhymes they read in the last lesson. Discuss how you might alter them to make a new version, e.g. *substitute your own rhyming nonsense phrase for 'ibble obble'; think of new phrases to replace 'long-legged'*

- With pupils, start working on a new counting rhyme. Add in some new nonsense words, (e.g. *swizzle, swozzle; higgle, hoggle*). Brainstorm some different words to rhyme with OUT.

- Make a list of the kind of actions you might have to go with your rhyme.

- Model reading the poem aloud as you write to check for rhythm and rhyme. Make changes as necessary as you go.

Group activities: differentiation

Working in pairs, all pupils should try to write an original playground rhyme using one of the models to help them. **Lower attainers** could continue with the work from shared writing, or continue with the skipping poem from the last lesson's group work (**PCM 69**).

Guided writing. Help pupils to hunt systematically through the alphabet for rhymes, making notes as they do so. Work on improving the rhythm.

Plenary

Listen to work in progress. Comment on the rhythm, rhyme and repetition. Ask pupils how easy the rhymes would be to remember.

EXTENDED WRITING

Pupils continue to work on their rhymes, revising and producing finished versions for a class collection.

YOU WILL NEED

- **Pupil's Book** pages 68–69
- Flipchart or blank OHT

⚠ WATCH OUT FOR

▶ Difficulty in sustaining rhythm and rhyme.

MAIN WRITING OBJECTIVE

- **To assemble and sequence points in order to plan the presentation of a point of view.**   4.3 T21

Word and sentence level objectives

- To reinforce work on prefixes and suffixes.   4.3 W8
- To spell words with common letter strings but different pronunciations.   4.3 W6

LESSON ONE

MODEL TEXT

- Explain the lesson objective: *to look at a book review.*

- Introduce the theme of favourite authors. Vote and note a few names on the board.

- Display and read 'My Favourite Author'. Do the children know the work of R L Stine? What sort of books does he write? Do they agree with the reviewer? Do they find his review persuasive?

- What does Daniel like about R L Stine's books? *they are spooky; there are lots of them*

- What does he tell us about it? *that it has really good descriptions; the setting; the characters; what the story is about; the bit he likes best; a favourite quote*

- Does this sound like the sort of book the children would like to read? Why or why not?

- Discuss how you might use the book blurb in writing the review – Daniel's review contains a real cliffhanger!

- Evaluate his review. Draw out one or two good and bad points. Briefly demonstrate by annotating the OHT.

Word and sentence level work

1 Ask pupils to find examples of prefixes in the text. *excellent, recommend*.

2 Can they find any suffixes? *mysterious, enormous, adventurous, recommendation, fiction, Abominable*

3 Explore the letter string spelling/pronunciation of *ou* in favourite, about, could, thought, coloured. Go on to investigate *ough* as in thought, through, cough, enough etc

Group activities: differentiation

Pupils complete the sentences on **PCM 70**. **Higher attainers** could also make a list of books by favourite authors. Use the school or class library to check titles and publishers where possible.

Plenary

Share responses. Add more authors to the list on the board. Prepare for homework by exploring briefly what they may dislike in stories.

YOU WILL NEED

- **Pupil's Book** page 70
- **OHT 39** – My Favourite Author
- **PCM 70** – Reading habits
- **PCM 71** – Homework

 ICT For activities linked to this lesson see **PAGE 108**

HOMEWORK

Use **PCM 71** to write about what they like and what they dislike in stories.

Pupil's Book page ● 70

Link to reading objectives

- To read further stories or poems by a favourite writer, making comparisons and identifying familiar features of the writer's work. 4.3 T9
- To describe and review own reading habits. 4.3 T10
- To investigate how style and vocabulary are used to convince the intended reader. 4.3 T18

Assumed prior knowledge

- To compare and evaluate books by the same author. 2.3 T4
- Book reviews. 3.3 T14

Planning suggestion

This unit would fit well into a school Book Week, or could form part of a series of lessons on specific authors. If possible, include a visit from a writer.

LESSON TWO

SHARED WRITING

- Explain the objective: *to make notes about a favourite author for presentation to an audience.*

- Decide on a writer who is generally popular with the class – perhaps the author of a recent class novel.

- Brainstorm the titles of some of his or her books.

- Look up the name of the publisher and make a note of it – most authors have one main publisher.

- Discuss where you might find out some facts about the writer e.g. blurbs, publishers' catalogues, books about authors (e.g. *Meet the Authors and Illustrators,* published by Puffin), websites such as Amazon.com

- Brainstorm some of the features that make the writer popular. Why do pupils enjoy their books? Who would they recommend them to?

- Ask pupils to contribute favourite moments or quotes from the writer's work.

- Briefly discuss how to use the notes in preparing a presentation. What props will pupils need? *books by author attractively displayed, bookmark for marking quotes etc*

YOU WILL NEED

- Book displays of popular authors
- Access to school library
- **OHT 40** – Notemaking frame
- **PCM 72** – Notemaking frame
- **Prompt Chart 8** – Point of view

Group activities: differentiation

Working in pairs, pupils plan an oral presentation about a favourite author. They should make notes on **PCM 72**. Explain that they may want 'props' – books, pictures, quotes etc. **Lower attainers** can use the notes from shared writing.

Guided writing. Check that pupils notes are clear, and cover the key points in a logical way

Plenary

Ask pairs of pupils to present their author and to describe what kind of props they will use in the final version.

EXTENDED WRITING

Pupils can continue to work on their notes for presentation and to prepare props. If possible, give the presentations in a school or class assembly.

WATCH OUT FOR

- Lack of logical sequence.
- Lack of convincing reasons for choosing the writer.

Information and Communication Technology

ICT and its place in the UK Curriculum

The curricula for England, Wales, Scotland and Northern Ireland all require that ICT should be used to support writing and learning about language. The Literacy Hour is an ideal starting place for many of these activities. By incorporating ICT activities into the Literacy Hour and other writing sessions, many elements of the ICT Programmes of Study may be taught in 'real' contexts.

The National Curriculum Orders for England & Wales, the new 5–14 Guidelines for Scotland and the Education Technology Strategy 1996–2000 in Northern Ireland, all give ICT a prominent place across all curriculum areas and give an entitlement for all pupils to achieve ICT capability.

ICT and Literacy

Literacy in the 21st century involves making sense of language and writing in many different contexts. In responding to texts, children must learn to recognise and be critical of the rich range of media; in producing their own writing, they must learn to use different media appropriately to suit their audience and purpose.

Children should be encouraged to explore the extent to which page-layout and design, use of colour, choice of fonts and text styles can enhance their writing. They also have opportunities, through the world wide web and multimedia authoring, to publish for wider audiences and to communicate via e-mail with children throughout the world.

During the Literacy Hour, pupils may be using ICT to support language and literacy development as well as developing their personal ICT capability.

Opportunities to develop the ICT skills associated with these activities can be included in the Literacy Hour and at other times throughout the week. The suggested activities provided in **Models for Writing** offer some starting points.

ICT to support whole class and group work

ICT can support and enhance discursive and interactive whole-class teaching and group work. The range of software available varies from fairly straightforward presentation packages available with standard office-type applications to fully-featured multimedia authoring tools. Interactive whiteboards, wide-format monitors, an LCD tablet with high-powered OHP, daylight projectors or large TV monitors should all be considered as options for presenting to groups. These vary considerably in price and are likely to represent significant capital investments for many primary schools. Teachers should discuss the options available with the ICT Co-ordinator or local advisory service.

When planning to use presentation software, consider what the 'added value' will be to pupils over traditional methods such as big books, flip-charts, blackboard and chalk, video, TV, radio, OHT, whiteboard and marker pen. A major advantage is that your presentation is stored in digital form and may be re-used for other purposes. If your presentation includes input from children during the session, this will also be stored for future use. Furthermore, a multimedia presentation allows a range of media to be used from one single workstation rather than juggling between an OHP, video and big book.

Models for Writing is accompanied by a set of colour OHTs which are an integral part of shared reading and writing. The OHTs contain extracts from model texts, and provide a wide variety of writing and planning frames to support pupils in developing their reading and writing skills. They allow the teacher to model both the reading and the writing processes to the class, and OHT pens can be used to highlight teaching points.

Audio-recording equipment is another valuable ICT tool. For example, when discussing performance poetry it may be used to enable children to experiment with different styles of delivery, evaluating each others' recordings.

Alternative input devices such as overlay keyboards, onscreen grids, touchscreens and voice input may be particularly useful to support young children who are not fully conversant with the QWERTY keyboard, or who need 'whole word' support for writing activities.

ICT for writing, editing and publishing

Using ICT to support children's writing means far more than simply asking them to word-process their text. The use of ICT can help children compose, transform and present text, and will give them a growing understanding and confidence in literacy, language, layout, style and design. Whether the writing and presentation of a text involves illustrating a poem, setting out information in a chart, or annotating a diagram, ICT can be used to support the activity and examples are provided in *Models for Writing*.

When writing, the children can change their work using various tools. Cutting and pasting paragraphs, sentences and words gives children the freedom to experiment with their text and decide the most appropriate way of ordering it. Using the electronic thesaurus allows the children to expand their vocabulary, and the spell-checker gives them the opportunity to check and correct their work. The final piece of writing will have a high standard of presentation that has been developed and adapted to suit the audience and the purpose of the piece.

As far as you are able, it is important to choose appropriate software for these activities. Some word-processing packages are capable of handling text and images to produce more sophisticated work, but if you want the children to begin to learn transferable skills associated with desktop publishing (DTP) you will achieve far better results with a desktop publishing program than with a word-processor.

Teachers who are confident with computers, and who have the appropriate painting or drawing software can also consider the use of ICT to illustrate children's work, where such an activity supports the learning objective.

Writing and the Internet

The Internet provides many opportunities for developing communication skills. Children should think about the emerging styles of writing which are appropriate for e-mail messages and be given opportunities to send and receive e-mail for real purposes. They may have 'net-pals' who will be interested in some of the writing arising from the activities in *Models for Writing*. Some of the activities lend themselves to setting up an e-mail project between schools in the UK using this scheme, or using a unit in the scheme as the starting point for a project with schools in other parts of the world.

Preparing some writing for the school website is another means whereby children will be writing for real and wider unknown audiences. There are two ways in which pupils may 'publish' on the web. They may have produced some writing for print which may be 'showcased' in a gallery on the school website. There may also be opportunities for children to design part of the school website or even their own website.

ICT and *Models for Writing*

On pages 102–108 you will find ICT activities for each unit of *Models for Writing*.

On pages 109–112 you will find a **Glossary of ICT terms**. This explains the ICT terminology used in the activities and gives simple, practical examples of what the terminology means.

Preparation and organisation of activities

In preparing to use ICT with *Models for Writing* teachers should check with the ICT Co-ordinator what hardware and software are available for use with Year 6. It is important to plan the development of ICT resources in consultation with other teachers, the Literacy Co-ordinator and ICT Co-ordinator. Many of the activities and resources prepared for use in one year group may be quickly modified for use by colleagues in other year groups if there is a school-wide policy on how to create and store digital material.

The ICT Co-ordinator will be able to advise on the most appropriate software to use for different applications, in particular when graphics are being created and stored.

Another important co-ordination function is to ensure that children have had the opportunity to learn the basic ICT skills they will need to use in order to carry out some of the activities suggested in *Models for Writing*.

The time taken to prepare the ICT activities for *Models for Writing* will depend on the ICT competence and confidence of teachers, as well as the software and hardware available in school. It may be appropriate for non-teaching assistants to do some of the preparatory tasks under the direction of a Year 6 teacher. Once the basic preparation is done, the resources will be available to, and may be modified and adapted for each class.

It is important to plan how to develop, save and back-up all ICT resources using a systematic and agreed filing structure either on floppy disks or a school network. Discuss the systems with the ICT Co-ordinator and develop a whole-school approach to managing digital resources.

IMPORTANT NOTE:

Several of the following ICT activities instruct you to prepare a text-file of the model text.

It is important to be aware that the keying in and electronic storage of copyright material is a breach of copyright law. The Publisher has obtained permission for the classroom activitites suggested in *Models for Writing*, but the keyed texts should not be stored on a network or otherwise transferred electronically.

If in doubt, consult your Copyright and Licensing Authority document.

Models for Writing: ICT activities

(Please note that these do not include the use of OHTs, which are within the main lesson plans for each unit.)

UNIT	TITLE	LESSON ONE	LESSON TWO
1	A Giant of a Man	Using a **graphics package** to create their own artwork, digital camera or clip-art collection, pupils illustrate a 'sympathetic' or 'unsympathetic' character, emphasising small details in their drawings. Prepare **word-banks** of adjectives and verbs to describe 'sympathetic' and 'unsympathetic', including those in the model texts.	Pupils may work in pairs or small groups, using the **word-banks**, to support writing character sketches for their illustrations.
2	Helping Each Other	Demonstrate how the use of 'outline' view in a word-processor or other planning software application provides useful support for planning writing, particularly when working with a response partner. Compare using ICT with other ways of planning to write together (e.g. brainstorming).	Prepare a **template** with a suitable collection of illustrations (clip-art or pupils' own work) and **text boxes** in a desktop publishing (DTP) package. Using 'outline' view in a word-processor or planning software application, pupils work in pairs to plan, revise and set out the tips for response partners. Pupils import the text into the template to draft and revise their list of tips, then save and print it as a poster for the wall.
3	The Magic Shoes	Prepare a story-board **template** and **word-bank** based on some of the ideas in children's spider diagrams. Demonstrate how to place text into the template. Using a talking word-processor, pupils will gain sound and text support to write their own story based on one of the spider diagrams. Demonstrate using cut, paste and copy.	Pupils continue to write and revise their stories, saving drafts and making use of the story-board **template** to structure the story. Print out an early draft of the story, and evaluate it with a partner. Split the story into paragraphs. Discuss the advantages of using a word-processor to plan, draft and revise stories.
4	Fantastic Mr Fox	Prepare a **text file** of Chapter 2 from OHT 6 with a **word-bank** for stage directions. Using a talking word-processor, pupils will gain sound and text support.	Prepare a **template** or **stylesheet** for playscript layout in a word-processor or desktop publishing (DTP) package. Pupils use the template and text file to re-write Chapter 2 as a playscript, concentrating on lively stage directions. Save and print copies to read aloud from. Revise the scripts and prepare a performance. Discuss the advantages of using ICT for re-drafting and making multiple copies of playscripts.

UNIT	TITLE	LESSON ONE	LESSON TWO
5	Feathers Fly!	Prepare a **template** in a desktop publishing (DTP) package with columns, **image boxes** and **text frames** suitable for newspaper layout.	Demonstrate how to use the \<shift\> key for speech marks. Using a talking word-processor, children write up their reports, using speech marks for direct quotes. Working in pairs, children revise and edit the stories, creating punchy headlines. Children import the copy into the DTP template, lay up the page and use suitable images to illustrate the report.
6	The Evacuee	Let the children explore a CD with other stories from evacuee children, cutting and copying text describing their feelings. Compare how these stories are told with the model text. Add to the list of informal or slang words used in the stories. Discuss how to reference material taken from the CD. Demonstrate how the use of 'outline' view in a word-processor or other planning software application provides useful support for planning stories.	Pupils work in pairs to plan a story in which they are evacuees. Pupils develop their outline to include direct speech, using speech marks, and copied, referenced text from the CD.
7	Up and Away!	Demonstrate how the use of 'outline' view in a word-processor or other planning software application provides useful support for planning paragraphs in a story. Using 'outline' view in a word-processor or planning software pupils work in pairs to plan a continuation and resolution of what happens to Philip.	Compare using ICT for planning a story with using PCMs or notebooks.
8	Cats sleep fat	Using a **graphics package** to create their own artwork, digital camera or clip-art collection, pupils prepare illustrations for their animal poem, thinking about particular characteristics in terms of what the animal is doing (verbs) and similes. Pupils write a description of their animal illustration, using powerful verbs and similes.	Working in pairs, pupils refine and revise their poems, save and print them with the illustration. This collection could form part of a class anthology.

UNIT	TITLE	LESSON ONE	LESSON TWO
9	Young Archaeologist	Prepare a **template** suitable for laying up a children's magazine in a desktop publishing (DTP) package with **image boxes**, **stylesheets** and **text frames**. Demonstrate how to achieve different styles for eye-catching effects: bulletted lists, numbered lists, font size, upper/lower case, centred text, bold text, colour. Pupils draft reports for the magazine, experimenting with different styles and effects to emphasise important points.	Pupils use the **template** to lay up their reports for the magazine. Save and print sample pages and discuss the different styles, comparing these with reports in commercially produced magazines and newspapers.
10	A Wolf in Me	Browse the **Internet** for sites with poetry anthologies and recommend a suitable selection with 'mood', 'feeling' and animal poems to the children. http://www.bbc.co.uk/education/listenandwrite/home.htm Prepare a **word-bank** of strong verbs and adverbs to describe mood and feelings.	Building on the anthology started in Unit 8, children write 'mood' poems using the **word-banks** as well as Yolande and Jeffery's poems as a model.
11	Weekend Bike Ride	This Unit provides a good introduction to work on modelling, where entering instructions to control a screen turtle 'tells' the computer how to carry out a procedure.	Using a version of LOGO to build on work done with floor turtles in Year 2, children should test out different sets of instructions on-screen. Discuss the language used to program the screen turtle and compare it with the instructional texts used to give directions for the bike ride. Bring out the importance of accuracy and detail when writing instructions for any purpose. Discuss the difference in use of verbs and adverbs when writing for people or to program a screen turtle.
12	The Iron Woman	Prepare a **text file** from PCM 32 (the Iron Woman emerging from the water) and **word-bank** from the model texts. Discuss how to use the first person and demonstrate using cut, paste and copy to revise the text. Using a talking word-processor, pupils will gain sound and text support to write their own descriptions.	Talk about how the story might develop, and how to write the next chapter Discuss the advantages of using a word-processor to plan, draft and revise stories.

UNIT	TITLE	LESSON ONE	LESSON TWO
13	How does it work?	Prepare a **template** with **image box** and set of **text boxes** in a desktop publishing (DTP) package. Demonstrate the use of text boxes, labelled diagrams, headings, short paragraphs and numbered points to present a clear explanation. Pupils use the template to draft and revise their explanations, based on the homework activity.	Encourage the children to concentrate on connectives and the sequence of the explanation. Save, print and test the explanation with another pupil. Discuss how the use of ICT makes revision to drafts, in the light of testing, easier.
14	The Emerald City of Oz	Let the children explore some fantasy games and simulations published on CD-ROM or DVD.	Ask them to think about how to distinguish between real and imaginary settings in this multimedia world. Compare how using other media (animation, sound, graphics), alongside text, extends the description of an imaginary setting. Discuss whether the use of other visual and aural media may limit our own imagination when writing and how to avoid this.
15	A Cautionary Tale	Browse the **Internet** for sites with poetry anthologies and recommend a suitable selection of cautionary tales to the children. http://www.bbc.co.uk/education/listenandwrite/home.htm Children make audio recordings of 'Henry King' and 'The Story of Augustus' as well as other cautionary tales, using pace, hysteria and melodrama as the tale reaches its climax.	Illustrate the poems and use a multimedia authoring package to create an audio-visual anthology of cautionary tales.
16	Robbers of the High Seas	This Unit offers a useful introduction to extending work on keyword searching. Select a suitable collection of CDs, DVDs or websites to support the class topic.	Demonstrate how to cut and paste relevant information into a word-processor. Help the children to identify keywords to refine searches for information to complete the 'What I need to know' section. Discuss how to reference the material collected. Demonstrate how to edit the material, cutting it down to notes, then building it up again into sentences.

UNIT	TITLE	LESSON ONE	LESSON TWO
17	Stories for Younger Children	Prepare a **template** in a desktop publishing (DTP) package with an **image box**, **text frames** and sample sentences for the Happy Families series. Using Mr Creep as a sample, write a Happy Families story for as many letters of the alphabet as possible.	Using a graphics package to create their own artwork, digital camera or clip-art collection, pupils illustrate each family. Save and print the stories and work with younger children to evaluate them.
18	Talking to Rod Theodorou	Non-fiction is also available in digital forms: on CD-ROM, DVD and the Internet. Discuss why the most up-to-date information about a particular subject may be found on a website. Discuss which websites are likely to have accurate information, and which may need some checking out to test the accuracy. After the children have completed the evaluation for a non-fiction book, compare the process with a relevant section from a CD or website.	Discuss presentation styles for non-fiction: for example headings, sub-headings, illustrated diagrams, short sentences, lists.
19	Snake and Lizard	Using 'outline' view in a word-processor or planning software pupils work in pairs to prepare notes for their fact-file using a range of information souces.	Expand the notes into a piece of extended writing, using the presentation styles discussed in other Units.
20	Red is like a trumpet sound	Prepare a **text file** of the model text: The Writer of this Poem. Prepare a **word-bank** of nouns and adjectives from the poem, selecting some that will rhyme, with additional words based on the class discussion. Demonstrate using cut, paste and copy.	Using a talking word-processor, pupils will gain sound and text support to write their own simile poem. Experiment with changing the lines to make the poem rhyme.
21	The Scrapyard of the Future	Pupils design a simple questionnaire to record numbers, text and choices to support a topic being studied by the class in another subject. Create a **database** with suitable fields and enter the data.	Demonstrate how the data may be displayed as pie charts or line graphs. Discuss the difference between these ways of presenting data, and making it informative.

UNIT	TITLE	LESSON ONE	LESSON TWO
22/23	Jason and the School Bully 1 Jason and the School Bully 2	These two Units should be treated together.	Let the children explore several 'branching stories' and adventure games on CD-ROM where they can make decisions about how the story or game develops. Based on their experience and understanding of the 'plot' and through study of *Jason and the School Bully*, discuss what factors influence decision-making and how authors plan stories to build up a character.
24	Its not fair!	Prepare a collection of statements in a word-processor, representing differing points of view about a particular topic of interest to the class. Prepare a **template** with two columns in a table.	Demonstrate how to select, drag and drop a statement into a cell in the table. Using the prepared collection of statements, sort them into two columns for and against the point of view. Use the lists of statements to write a presentation of one point of view.
25	It wasn't a brick . . .	Prepare a **text file** and **word-bank** of the model text. Using a talking word-processor, pupils will gain sound and text support to write their own story ending for Sausage's dive.	Demonstrate using cut, paste and copy. Talk about how the new story ending affects the beginning of the story. Go back to the model text and write an alternative beginning, to match the new ending. Discuss the advantages of using a word-processor to plan, draft and revise stories.

UNIT	TITLE	LESSON ONE	LESSON TWO
26	Special Offer!	Prepare sample texts of advertisements and associated word-banks: for sale, wanted, special offer etc.	Demonstrate how to achieve different styles in a word-processor: bulleted lists, font size, upper/lower case, centred text, bold text, colour. Using a talking word-processor, pupils should experiment with different layouts for their advertisement, thinking carefully about choice of words and presentation. Pupils should save and print each layout as a basis for group or class discussion about appropriate use of styles and language.
27	Childhood Tracks	Make audio recordings of the sense poems, using a range of sound effects. Illustrate the poems and use a multimedia authoring package to create an audio-visual anthology of sense poems.	
28	I'm writing to ask . . .	Prepare a **word-bank** including persuasive phrases and words. Children use the word-bank and talking word-processor to write the first draft of a persuasive letter on a topic of interest to them. Discuss how to improve the letter, and revise it.	Save and print the final version. Send the letter, and await the reply!
29	Skipping, Clapping and Counting	Using a drawing or painting package, create abstract designs which may be used to illustrate the playground rhyming poems. Pupils explore using these abstract designs as repeating patterns to form 'wallpaper' behind the playground rhymes.	
30	My Favourite Author	Browse some of the online bookshops such as http://amazon.co.uk/ which publish book reviews and interviews with authors. Pupils may submit reviews online for the world to share.	

Glossary of ICT terms

All teachers will need to understand and use the vocabulary associated with ICT and help children to use it appropriately and in context.

This list provides a broad summary of terms and acronyms which will be needed to provide support for children at Key Stage 2.

Address: the unique identifier for a web page. Typically an address takes the form http://www.repp.co.uk and should be entered into the address bar on the browser window. In this example, <repp.> is the name of the company owning the website, <co.> indicates that it is a company (others include <org.> for organisation, <gov.> for government, <sch.> for school, <ac.>for university etc.) and <uk> indicates the country. No country code usually indicates a US based website or a site, which regards itself as international.

Application: a piece of software, usually installed onto the computer or run over a network.

Attachment (see enclosure): a file sent with an e-mail message. An attachment may be text, graphics or sound. It may be helpful to imagine them as 'paper-clipped' to a file as a note may be attached to a paper document.

Authoring software (see presentation software): an application which enables the user to create documents using mixed media including text, still and moving images, and sound, with a means of moving between pages or screens. These packages may be used to produce presentations for use in the classroom or hall, as well as for creating web pages.

Back up: to make copies of documents or applications on another disk or tape as a safeguard against data loss. It is essential to keep regular back ups. Check the school policy with the ICT Co-ordinator.

Bookmark (see favourite): to store the address of a web page in a list in order to return to it during another session browsing the world wide web.

Browse: to move from page to page on a website or CD-ROM.

Browser software: an application which displays the pages of a website. The two major browser applications are Microsoft *Internet Explorer* and *Netscape Navigator*.

Clip art: images available commercially or as free collections distributed on disks, CD-ROM or the Internet, which may be incorporated into documents, multimedia presentations and websites.

Cut and paste: to move text or images from a document and place them in another part of the same document or into another document.

Database software: an application which enables the user to set up fields and records containing data, and to sort the data and display the information in a number of ways including graphs and charts.

Daylight projector: a piece of equipment which projects the display from a computer onto an external screen. The projectors may be wall- or ceiling-mounted or stand-alone portable devices.

DTP (desktop publishing) software: an application which enables the user to combine text and graphics, using templates for page-layout and styles. Text and graphics are typically placed in text or picture frames after having been originally created in word-processing, text-editing, painting or drawing packages.

Digital: information which is held in numerical form. Typically, in a computer, this is as a sequence of binary numbers.

Directory: a folder on the desktop which contains documents and sub-directories enabling users to organise their work, and find documents and applications easily. The directory system is often likened to a filing cabinet, with drawers, sub-divisions and folders.

Document: a single piece of work. A document may be in a word-processor, desktop publisher or database application. Each document must be saved with a unique filename.

Download: to save material such as text, images or software from another computer, the Internet or a network, and store it locally for future use on a hard disk or school network.

E-mail (electronic mail): a service provided on the Internet whereby electronic messages may be sent by one user to one or many other users throughout the world in a few minutes at minimal cost. In order to use e-mail, users will need to have e-mail software and a profile set up which includes a personal e-mail address.

Enclosure (see attachment): a file sent with an e-mail message. An enclosure may be text, graphics or sound.

Favourite (sometimes spelled favorite, see bookmark): to store the address of a web page in a list in order to return to it during another session browsing the world wide web.

Filename: the name used when saving a document as a file. It is important to use filenames that you and others will understand when sharing documents on a network or creating collections of digital resources.

Font: a set of type characters in the same style. A font will include different weights (bold, light, book) and different slants (italic, oblique). There are numerous fonts, some will be supplied with each application, others may be purchased or obtained from free collections.

Graphic: an image or picture.

Hyperlink: the electronic link to related information (text, graphics, sound, entire documents, whole pages or websites) which enables users to browse the Internet or a CD-ROM by making their own choices about routes through the material. The cursor will usually change from an arrow to, for example, a hand icon when it is over a hyperlink. Hyperlinks are often highlighted in some way such as underlining. Clicking on a hyperlink takes the user to the related page or website.

Image box (or image frame): the placeholder for a graphic, picture or image in a document.

Interactive whiteboard: a large, touch-sensitive board onto which an image of the computer desktop is projected. Users can interact with the projected image by drawing on the board with a stylus.

ISP (Internet service provider): the company providing Internet services such as e-mail and access to the world wide web for a school, organisation, business or household. Some ISPs do not charge for their services but may carry advertising. Check with your ICT Co-ordinator how to access Internet services from school.

Internet: the network of networks. Networks are formed by connecting computers. The Internet has been formed by connecting networks into a global network of networks. It provides a set of protocols which allow different networks to talk to each other, and services such as e-mail and the world wide web.

Intranet: a closed, private network or network of networks which uses the same protocols as the Internet and provides the same services such as e-mail.

LCD (liquid crystal display) panel: a flat screen display which can be used with a high powered overhead projector for presentations to groups.

Multimedia: the presentation of information through the use of more than one medium e.g. text, sound, images.

Network: formed by connecting computers in order to share files and applications. Networks are either peer-to-peer where any computer can talk to any other computer on the network or client/server where one computer holds all the files and applications and can be accessed by the client computers.

Optical character recognition (OCR) software: an application which enables a scanner to 'read' text and convert it into a digital form. Once saved, the text may be exported to a word-processor for editing.

PDF (portable document format): a proprietary document file format, for which a reader is freely available from Adobe, which has been designed to ensure that documents, particularly DTP documents retain all their formatting and typographic styles and effects when viewed on another computer.

Presentation software (see authoring software): an application which enables the user to create documents using mixed media including text, still and moving images and sound with a means of moving between pages or screens. These packages may be used to produce presentations for use in the classroom or hall.

Scanner: a piece of equipment which enables users to copy paper-based materials such as photographs or illustrations and save them in digital format. A scanner produces a bitmap image composed of pixels and works in a similar way to a photocopier. Many scanners include OCR software as standard.

Search engine: a service provided commercially on the Internet used to search for documents on the Internet. Users access the search engine from a web page on the providers website by entering key words. The service is usually free to the user and paid for by advertising.

Spell-checker: a function available in most word-processors and many other software applications which enables users to check spelling. It is important to remember that spell-checkers use a dictionary stored on the computer and will search it for logical matches. Users will need a certain basic level of spelling strategies to be able to make use of this facility. A spell-checker will not pick up mis-spelt words that are in the wrong context (for example, 'there' and 'their'). Some software has grammar checkers which teachers should consider using with care. Check what conventions are used. The problem with many grammar and spell-checker software is that is uses US English, although there may be opportunities to customise the dictionaries.

Stylesheet (see also template): 'blank' documents which may be saved to include margins, text styles, headers, footers, page-numbering, guidelines, image frames and text boxes amongst many other features which may be set up so that every page has a common format.

Table: a function available in some word-processors and spreadsheets to organise lists into tables. These may then be sorted according to various criteria such as date, alphabetical order, number etc. Tables should be used in preference to the <tab> key when putting lists into a word-processor.

Talking word-processor: speech output is available in some word-processing packages. The user may hear individual letters, words or complete sentences as they are keyed in, or on demand. This is very valuable as support for reading and writing activities.

Template: 'blank' documents which may be saved to include margins, text styles, headers, footers, page-numbering, guidelines, image frames and text boxes amongst many other features which may be set up so that every page has a common format. They are essential for use in desktop publishing packages and useful for word-processing. When writing more than a short paragraph, it is 'good practice' to set up styles for the entire document rather than make 'local' changes to, for example, centre and embolden a heading.

Text file: any file which contains plain text. When transferring text between different applications and computer platforms, it is advisable to select rich text format (RTF) from the save options.

Text frame (text box): the placeholder for text in a desktop publishing document.

Thesaurus: a function available in many word-processing applications for finding a synonym, an antonym, or related words for a selected word in the user's text.

Typing tutor: an application which trains users to touch type, typically using a structured 'drill' approach with on-screen copy to practise typing from.

Undo: a useful feature available in most software applications. Reverses the last action and may be used more than once in some applications to retrace a series of actions.

Website: a collection of pages published on the world wide web.

Word count: a function available in many word-processing applications for automatically counting the number of words, pages, characters and lines in a selected part of the document or the entire document.

Word-bank: a collection of words, customised by the user and stored in a word-processor. Many word-processors designed for the education market have word-bank facilities whereby selected groups of words and phrases may be saved and used to support writing. Check with the documentation in the program available for how to create and save word-banks.

Word-processing software: an application which enables users to manipulate text.

World wide web: an Internet service which provides information in the form of pages which can include text, images, video clips and sound. These are viewed using a web browser.